746.97
W8.

SOFT COVERS
For
HARD TIMES

SOFT COVERS

For

HARD TIMES

Quiltmaking
&
The Great Depression

MERIKAY WALDVOGEL

Introduction by Robert Cogswell

Photography by David Luttrell

RUTLEDGE HILL PRESS
Nashville, Tennessee

Published in Nashville, Tennessee, by Rutledge Hill Press, Inc., 513 Third Avenue South, Nashville, Tennessee 37210.

Typography by Bailey Typography, Inc.
Design by Harriette Bateman, Studio Six.

Library of Congress Cataloging-in-Publication Data

Waldvogel, Merikay, 1947-
    Soft covers for hard times : quiltmaking & the Great Depression /
Merikay Waldvogel ; introduction by Robert Cogswell ; photography by
David Luttrell.
        p.   cm.
    Includes bibliographical references.
    ISBN 1-55853-062-2 $22.95
    1. Quilts—United States—History—20th century.   2. United
States—Social conditions—1933-1945.   I. Title.
NK9112.W35   1990   90-32002
746.9'7'097309043—dc20   CIP

1 2 3 4 5 6 7 8 — 96 95 94 93 92 91 90
Printed in Singapore through Palace Press

CONTENTS

For Jerry

ILLUSTRATIONS

The Soft Covers for Hard Times exhibition is sponsored by the Knoxville Museum of Art, Knoxville, Tennessee.

PREFACE

On a brisk autumn morning in Chicago in 1974, I entered an antique quilt store and emerged minutes later with a quilt under my arm. I was surprised at how quickly it all had happened, and I remember thinking that this quilt had talked to me. It was not a typical quilt, and I liked that: it was curiously haphazard rather than symmetrical, and it was dark brown and green rather than in pastels. I knew it would go with my new loom and hanging ferns in my studio apartment.

I have often wondered what drew me to an antique quilt store that day. Why did buying the quilt seem like the right thing to do? Now I know. A quilt revival was taking place—the second one of the twentieth century! I did not grow up with quilts on my bed. In fact, I had never seen anyone do any quilting. Even though I thought I was being a nonconformist by buying a quilt, I was merely getting in step with a growing band of quilt enthusiasts who were collecting and making quilts.

In the early 1970s conditions were right for a renewal of interest in quilts and quiltmaking. Women in rural areas had continued to quilt, but urban and suburban women tempted by all sorts of new streamlined gadgets to fill their modern homes had stopped quilting. Quilting was viewed as old-fashioned and therefore out-of-date; but in the 1960s a strong back-to-earth movement began, and with it came a renewed interest in women's traditional crafts. When the Whitney Museum of Art in New York City mounted an exhibit of antique quilts in 1971, suddenly quilts were not only accepted as craft, but also as an art form. Since then books, national magazines, quilt museums, quilting conferences, and antique quilt stores have fed the desire for information about quiltmaking and quilt collecting; and the trend shows no sign of dying out very soon.

Today it is not unusual to see an antique quilt in a modern office. Try to imagine how confused a quilt historian or an archaeologist might be in the twenty-first century when contemplating that phenomenon. Why didn't this career woman buy a piece of modern art that reflected the highly developed technology of her time? This seeming contradiction is at the heart of the exhibition of Depression era quilts. Why do these quilts not reflect the hard times of the 1930s?

In the Colonial Revival of the 1920s, quilts, too, gained the attention of artists and historians. Suddenly the quilt form was no longer just a warm blanket; it was decorative and was imbued with historical importance. In fact, it reflected the soft, prosperous times of the 1920s. Textile mills produced a wide variety of pretty fabrics, and women had the money to purchase them. When the hard times hit, the soft, pastel colors for quilts continued to be promoted in women's magazines. And therein is the story of *Soft Covers for Hard Times*.

I think we can learn something about ourselves and our society by comparing the current quilt revival to the earlier one. I am fascinated by the interplay of corporations and quiltmakers: corporations trying to come up with something new and women trying to spend as little as possible.

For the most part, quit historians have ignored twentieth-century quilts, asking, "What is there to know?" I felt the same way; and when Bets Ramsey and I began the Tennessee quilt survey in 1984, we chose a cutoff date of 1930 because we felt quilts made after 1930 were nationalized. We were more interested in regional quilt traditions. Other state quilt project coordinators envied our decision not to document quilts made after 1930, but I feared we had missed an important piece of quilt history in Tennessee. I must admit that the thought of documenting hundreds of 1930s quilts did not thrill me at the time.

When the Knoxville Museum of Art proposed a quilt exhibit on "Depression Era Quiltmaking of Tennessee" to coincide with the National Quilting Association Convention in Knoxville in 1990, I had my opportunity to make amends.

I talked with a history professor at the University of Tennessee about Depression-era social programs in Tennessee, thinking he would be interested in quilts made by wives of black workers at construction projects of the Tennessee Valley Authority (TVA). I began by giving him a brief overview of quilt history and told him how the pretty pastel quilts of the 1930s began to appear all over the country in the 1920s and 1930s. They all looked very similar, but this TVA quilt was something special. He listened intently but said, "Go back to the pretty pastel quilts and ask yourself why they got that way. That is what fascinates me." He said the same homogenization phenomenon occurred in traditional music, folklore, and crafts in the 1930s. He encouraged me to investigate what forces affected the form and substance of quilts.

So that became the question: Why were Depression-era quilts generally pretty and generally the same all over the country? What made them so soft in the cruel context of the hard times of the 1930s?

My research has been an interesting search full of intrigue, suspense, and luck. I began by interviewing women who quilted during the Depression to find out what kinds of quilts they were making and where they got their materials and patterns. I searched for their quilt patterns in the magazines, catalogs, and newspapers of the 1930s. Especially interesting were the *Good Housekeeping* articles by Tennessee's own nationally known quilt designer, Anne Orr. I knew the Sears National Quilt Contest had an important impact on quiltmaking in the 1930s, so I checked the local accounts in Tennessee's major newspapers. I even interviewed flour company executives and heard about the fierce battle between paper and cloth bag manufacturers. In the end, I chose thirty quilts to tell the diverse story of quiltmaking in Tennessee; but this exhibit is not just about Tennessee quilts. Except for climatic conditions that allowed Tennessee women to grow cotton for their batting, Tennessee women made quilts the same way women in other parts of the country did.

Many people helped in my search for answers. I especially thank the men and women who shared their memories of the Great Depression and quiltmaking. Without the generosity and faith of the people who have lent their quilts and artifacts to the exhibit, the complete story would not have been told.

The staff of the Knoxville Museum of Art, especially former director Rebecca Massie Lane, Leigh Hendry, Lisa Simpson, Jeanne Fulkerson, Sarah Kramer, Kenny Jones and Joyce Gralak, have enthusiastically supported my efforts even when times got rough.

My friends from Smoky Mountain Quilters, especially Linda Claussen, Eva Earle Kent, Jean Lester, Sue Jenkins, and Becky Harriss, helped with book photography and exhibit preparation of the quilts.

I am most grateful to David Luttrell and his staff for providing the high quality color photographs included herein. To Margaret Luttrell, again, my thanks for advice on the still life photography.

Special thanks go to Roby Cogswell, director of folk arts for the Tennessee Arts Commission, who kept me focused, came up with the title, and agreed to write an introduction to this book.

I would also like to thank a number of libraries and their staffs for help with the research: The John C. Hodges Library of the University of Tennessee, Knoxville, especially the Special Collections, Reference Department, and Microforms Department; the Lawson-McGhee Library of Knox County, Tennessee, especially the McClung Collection; the Nashville Public Library, especially the Nashville Room; the Tennessee State Library and Archives; Fisk University Library; and the Sears, Roebuck and Company Archives of Business History.

I want to especially thank quilt researcher Cuesta Benberry who has compiled information on almost every aspect of this book. She graciously shared the information, spent time talking with me, and encouraged me to dig deeper.

I would also like to thank another quilt researcher, Barbara Brackman, for sharing her information on the Sears, Roebuck and Company national quilt contest.

Jeanne Webb, Gedy Higgins, Jean Dubois, Mildred Locke, and Ruth Neitzel were all interested in different aspects of Anne Orr's work. Their information forms the foundation of the chapter on Anne Orr, and I thank them.

The chapter on Tennessee Valley Authority quilts evolved from a Women's History Month quilt exhibition I curated in March 1986. At that time, a high ranking TVA employee, Elizabeth Brown, shared a 1934 memo in which Dr. J. Max Bond reported on quiltmaking by wives of black construction workers at Wheeler Dam. I am grateful to Nan Scott, Director of the TVA Federal Women's Program, and to Patricia Barnard, a TVA historian. Several retired TVA employees, especially Ruth Martinson and Walter Goldston, provided important clues to the whereabouts of the quiltmakers and designers. In the end, I enjoyed many pleasant and productive hours with the quilt designer Ruth Clement Bond, her husband Dr. J. Max Bond, and daughter Jane Bond-Howard. I thoroughly enjoyed my interviews with Grace Tyler and Rose Marie Thomas, makers of the TVA quilts. I thank them all from the bottom of my heart for their faith in my endeavors.

Anna Cook of Germantown, Tennessee, may have the most comprehensive collection of cotton sacks and related artifacts in the world. She is as intrigued with sacks and their history as I am with quilts, and in the 1930s sacks and quilts became intimately linked. I thank her for finding me. The exhibit items selected from her collection add immeasurably to a better understanding of domestic life in the 1930s.

Finally, I want to thank my friend Bets Ramsey, with whom I wrote *The Quilts of Tennessee: Images of Domestic Life Prior to 1930*. Several of the quilts and the stories mentioned in this book were located during the Quilts of Tennessee survey conducted from February 1984 through July 1985. Bets Ramsey has encouraged many people to write down quilt history and, more importantly, to share it with the public. I thank her for encouraging me.

INTRODUCTION

From Making Do to How-To

From the hindsight of half a century, the Great Depression looms as a cultural watershed, not only in American history but even more so in the casual, intimate sense of the past by which families and communities take stock of who they are and how they got to be that way. The distinction of having lived through the Depression is a badge of experience and seniority that has since separated adult generations and their outlooks on success, necessities, and materialism. And for children of postwar years, coming to an understanding of hard times past has been essential to understanding their elders' psyches and answering questions of their own prehistory. As firsthand memories of the Depression recede, physical heirlooms and mental hand-me-downs assume increasing importance in relating us to this critical period of modern history.

Few surviving artifacts are so closely connected to the experience of the Depression—functionally and symbolically—as are quilts preserved from the era. During hard times, the quilt was a homemade comfort in homes where comforts were often scarce. The Depression threatened the economic foundations of American families, raising the specters of lost jobs, homes, and farms and forcing most households to adopt strategies of self-denial and resourcefulness. It was a time for scrimping and getting by, making do or doing without, finding things to fall back on. To housewives striving to eke out bare necessities, the impulse to quilt was a culturally inherited survival instinct.

On the eve of the 1930s, the old-fashioned pattern of home life in which quilting was an essential, practical activity was well on its way to extinction. The causes of the Depression were bound up in America's movement from an agrarian to an industrial society, which created unprecedented dependence upon the uncertainties of a market economy.[1] Industrialism wrought profound changes on daily life in the American home: electrical, gas, and water lines linked households to service infrastructures; manufactured goods filled needs for food, clothing, and furnishings; life was made easier—and different—by the automobile, washing and sewing machines, radio, motion pictures, and dozens of other inventions and modern conveniences. While such amenities were most closely associated with cities, their influence spread far into the countryside as well, with mail-order merchandising via Rural Free Delivery introducing farm families to mass consumer culture.[2]

The 1920s were years of prosperity and change in household life, in contrast to the hard times that followed. Having adapted their lives to ready-made commodities and work-saving luxuries, many mainstream Americans became unable to afford them when the Depression happened. For them, getting by in the Depression meant relearning some of the self-reliance of preindustrial times, dusting off obsolete ways of doing things for themselves. For those whose lives had remained close to folk culture, the times were still hard; but the adjustments were less extreme.

If traditional folklife offered practical recourse to those facing desperation in the 1930s, it had inspirational and symbolic importance as well. Old-timey know-how suggested American solutions to an American crisis. Folkways had direct continuity with pioneer days, when they had provided the means for overcoming lowly beginnings and similar daily hardships. Bringing to mind the frontier past and the virtues of perseverance, folk culture positively evoked the core national value of rugged, determined individualism.

Underlying the investment of folkways with such symbolic meaning was a long-standing intellectual aversion to the mechanized, impersonal workings of industrial society. In the nineteenth century, British philosopher-writers William Morris and John Ruskin had urged rejection of the machine age and a return to nobler sensibilities and ways of living congruent with quality handwork. Among practicing artists, their precepts inspired the Arts and Crafts Movement, while antiquarian aspects of their ideas fueled romantic nationalist activity throughout Europe, cultivating new respect for folk art and folklife.[3] By the turn of the century, such sentiments influenced American efforts to articulate pride in our national cultural past. The so-called Colonial Revival, which coalesced growing interests in historic Americana, gained full public display at the 1893 Chicago World's Fair.[4] An inaccurate hodge-podge of nostalgic elements, the Colonial Revival primarily influenced architecture, but it also encompassed interests in such wide-ranging facets of folk culture as farm artifacts, handicrafts, interior furnishings, and cookery.

By the Depression, the labels *colonial* and *early American* symbolically linked to our national identity all kinds of traditional things and traditional ways of doing things. As a focal point for American romantic nationalism, folklife came to play a role in the New Deal strategies for addressing the problems of the Depression. Documentation of folk culture emerged as a subtheme of programs in the Works Progress Administration: the Federal Writers Project employed out-of-work literary talent to commit Americana to paper, with attention to legend, folklore, and regional traditions; the Federal Music Project included ambitious efforts to collect living folk music from all parts of the country; and the Federal Art Project initiated, among other things, the *Index of American Design,* which lent aesthetic credibility to folk art.[5] More rigorously detailing what, in fact, American traditions were, these efforts reflected the conviction that fostering pride and confidence in our national identity was central to the mission of recovery.

Whether or not they were actually born of the hardest necessity and worn by the heaviest use, Depression quilts have exuded meanings and assumptions associated with the simplest patchworks that embodied such circumstances. The quintessential Depression quilt was a product of folk culture revitalized by the times. An extension of an organic tradition, it was based on traditional patterns, aesthetics, and techniques handed down informally within family or community; and it was produced through intensive work, largely out of materials at hand. There were inevitably store-bought components like thread, but resourceful quilters "made do" by salvaging cloth from used clothes, curtains, and other household fabrics—such scavenging being an ultimate enactment of Depression values—and procuring cotton direct from the field for batting. The patchwork top was colorful and stylized according to the background and individuality of the quilter, who displayed her skill and ingenuity in the design and the quilting. Despite these artistic elements, quilts were not made just for show. They were working bedcovers, and their utility accounted for much of their symbolism. Created by loving hands, Depression quilts were maternal artifacts providing warmth, protection, and solace, domestic needs that were heightened during hard times. None of the symbolism, of course, was new; but the Depression intensified the quilt's significance as an icon of the womanly role in the home.

Today, the symbolism bound up in quilts as Depression artifacts underlies oral history concerning particular quilts and quilting experiences from the period. Cherished textiles spur recollections about the times, the circumstances, and the makers. Common elements in these accounts serve emblematic purposes, as the artifacts testify to hardships endured, the self-sacrifice and dedication of the quilter, and lives of family members who had worn the fabrics before they were turned into patchwork. But just as the archetypal profile of the Depression quilt is not accurately borne out in every quilt produced in the era, so stories of quilting in the Depression reveal a surprising diversity in the social, artistic, and economic details of how and why the quilts were made.

Louise Edelman, for example, vividly recalls very different details from Depression quilting in Kentucky:

> My mother, Ida Atchison Rhorer, pieced the top for the winning quilt in the [1933] Chicago Exposition. Sears, Roebuck and Company gave the prize of one thousand dollars, and it went to Margaret Caden, who entered the quilt. The Caden Art Shop in Lexington sold all kinds of fancy work. It was parceled out by the piece to be made by various persons who worked for Miss Caden. My mother was one of those.
>
> The rules of the contest were that one individual would design the pattern, cut the pieces, sew them together by hand, finish her quilt top, put in her batting and back, quilt it herself, and then bind it—all the work to be done by one person. This wasn't followed, however. Miss Caden gave my mother the pattern I think she'd assembled from several different ones she had, and the fabric, and asked her to cut it out and piece it together. I don't know who put the binding on it. It could have been the quilters. Mother didn't get more than probably twenty-five dollars for the piecing. Sometimes she got fifteen dollars for a simple piece. Mother kept some of the scraps, and I still have them and one quilt square.
>
> When the contest [winner] was announced, of course, it was widely publicized, and mother saw it in the paper. She knew it was her work. She knew what the rules were. Other ladies did the quilting, also on contract work for Miss Caden. My mom knew it wasn't fair, but she never said anything about it. Miss Caden—both Miss Margaret

and Miss Caroline—were aristocratic ladies of Lexington. I'm sure they sold a lot of quilts to those horse folks who came into town. The women who worked for them, it was Depression times, and they had to have their jobs. That was the reason my mother kept her mouth shut.[6]

Ida Rhorer's experience reveals some of the facts of Depression quilting that have been obscured. Accurately appraising the quilts of the 1930s requires tempering romanticism with some of these harder realities as well.

As some WPA programs documented folk traditions, other private and governmental efforts, especially in the South, promoted folk arts for social and economic motives. The southern Appalachian region in particular had been mythologized for decades as a place where folklife was linked with poverty and substandard living conditions. Consistent with the romanticized notions of the Colonial Revival, other Americans regarded southern mountaineers as "our contemporary ancestors."[7] Retention of folk arts was often seen as evidence that Appalachian people remained untouched by modern society. One of the foremost early books on quilting stressed the connection:

The art of quilt-making is still widely practiced in the southern mountains where life is still as simple and un-hurried as it was a century ago. The mountain women still make their original patterns and have no conception of life as lived in a twentieth-century city.[8]

Quilting and other folk arts, of course, were practiced elsewhere as well, but Appalachia cornered the mystique. Church missions and settlement schools had encouraged this conception in making the revival and outside marketing of handicrafts key elements in their attempts to gain improvements for the mountain people.[9] The movement helped turn folk craft objects into saleable commodities; and such quaint, nostalgic associations appealed to potential buyers, who were largely urban, northern, wealthy, and detached from folk culture themselves.

Pre-Depression craft activity not only created demand but also marketing networks for handicrafts. Urban craft stores, commission work agents, mail order services, bulk resale, and the first tourist sale outlets were all parts of the system by the 1920s. If such arrangements helped settlement school craft industries generate income for social betterment, there were profits to be made by private enterprise as well. For every altruistic craft program in the South there was also an entrepreneur exploiting the discrepancy between the low pay expectations of isolated craftspeople and the elevated prices for quality handwork in distant markets.

Among these for-profit ventures, cottage industries in quilting and other needlework, such as the one run by Margaret Caden in Lexington, Kentucky, were especially extensive and well-organized.[10]

Governmental programs also encouraged quilting for home use rather than for sale. Along with the virtues of busy hands saving household money, the social aspects of quilting bees bringing people together appealed to New Deal sensibilities. Although crafts were not programwide priorities, local quilting initiatives were conducted under both the Resettlement Administration (later the Farm Security Administration) in communities created for farmers relocated from exhausted land and the Tennessee Valley Authority, in workers' communities associated with dam construction projects.

More influential in stimulating domestic quilting was the work of home demonstration agents in county Agricultural Extension Service offices. While these professional home economists were already active in the South, the Depression increased both their numbers and interest in their advice and services. The agents sought to improve the quality of life for farm families by teaching progressive home management, which sometimes placed them in an adversarial position to folk culture. If folk culture proved immune to outright change, the agents attempted subtle modifications. As nutritionists, for example, they were careful to encourage beneficial aspects of folk cookery while discouraging traditional foods considered unhealthy. As promoters of grassroots quilting, home demonstration agents no doubt spurred great productivity; but by advocating innovations, they were also significant catalysts for change in the quilters' craft.

Quilting was changing during the 1930s, succumbing through the influence of mass media and mass marketing to the process by which an overreaching national popular culture has eroded American folk traditions and regional folk cultures. Well before the Depression, the wide dissemination of quilt patterns in print—through magazines like *Farm and Fireside,* syndicated newspaper columns, and pattern books—was altering the dynamics of traditional quilting, just as records and radio were dramatically accelerating the circulation of folk music styles and repertoires.[11] Folk quilters, once limited to traditionally inherited patterns, were increasingly exposed to unfamiliar designs from impersonal outside sources, some traditional patterns from elsewhere, and others entirely new. Printed sources encouraged experimentation and novelty; and, as with printed recipes promoted by makers of food products, the companies printing patterns often had their own gadgets, fabric, or notions to sell. Publications also expanded the group consciousness of quilters, who began to see themselves less within isolated local circles and more within a nationwide community of needleworkers.

Sears, Roebuck and Company's 1933 Century of Progress quilt contest took full advantage of this national network. Contests were an emerging popular culture phenomenon that publicly institutionalized American competitiveness. Beauty, music, recipe, marathon dance, and even preaching contests proliferated in the years of the Depression. Quilt contests had begun in the nineteenth century, and there had even been previous national competitions, but nothing approached the scale or promotional significance of the Century of Progress contest.[12] It closely followed the plan of the Ford Motor Company's 1926 old-time fiddle contest, with local and regional prizes linking grassroots dealerships to the national finals and with the solid values evoked by a traditional art form enhancing the image of the sponsor.[13] Depression times and impressive prize money insured a glut of contestants; nearly 25,000 quilts were entered.[14] With Sears ostensibly offering female customers an opportunity to realize the American dream of self-made success and exhibiting winners at their Chicago World's Fair pavilion, the contest was a stroke of public relations genius.

Considering the number of consumers from rural backgrounds, relating folk arts to marketing made good sense, and Sears was by no means the only company to do so. Flour manufacturers made wide use of the folk arts connection, finding radio broadcasts of traditional music to be ideal advertising in their regional markets. In fact, the patronage of such firms helped popularize a number of folk music styles: in Louisville, Ballard Flour Mills' sponsorship of the Ballard Chefs, beginning in the 1920s, gave respectability to Afro-American jug band music[15]; Fort Worth's Burrus Mills began a sponsorship in 1931 that, through the legendary Light Crust Doughboys, launched the western swing style[16]; and as late as the 1950s Nashville's Martha White Mills linked its name to bluegrass through their association with Flatt & Scruggs and the Foggy Mountain Boys.[17]

Naturally mindful of housewives, flour companies seized on the promotional potential of quiltmaking in the Depression when they discovered that empty flour sacks were being cut up for quilt pieces. Plain muslin with indelible marking was replaced with bright prints and detachable paper labels, and sack suppliers diversified their output to appeal to quilters. Although price was still an object, Depression quilters began purchasing their flour with the sack in mind. Thus, in a time of need, they may have ironically initiated the marketing institution of stressing package over product.

Marketing objectives clearly motivated Sears' Century of Progress quilt contest, and they also prevailed in the judging. The organizers were vague—and some contestants were disgruntled—about the actual judging standards.[18] Whether the the rules clearly spoke to the point or not, grassroots quilters were ethically justified in assuming that entries ought to have been conceived and made by the contestant herself. But apparently Sears, which would gain the right to sell patterns and kits for winning entries, was simply looking for good quilts that would appeal to prevailing tastes in the quilt revival and that housewives would be tempted to copy.

Somehow it never became an issue that the winner, Margaret Caden, was not really a quilter, but a quilt designer and seller, and that the needlework in her entry was not her own. Given her background, she was in a perfect position to successfully anticipate the operative aesthetics of the contest. The winning quilt was her own version of a traditional star-motif pattern, with stuffed feathers added in the quilting—striking but replicable by any accomplished quilter. Referred to in connection with the contest as "Star of the Century" among other names, it was later sold in Sears kits and patterns as "Feathered Star." The Mountain Mist company also subsequently marketed the design as "Star of the Bluegrass."[19]

Traditionally, quilters had freely worked variations into inherited designs, the better ones contributing something of themselves to the common stream of tradition. But as business considerations and marketing rights entered the picture, traditional elements of quilting, like those in other folk arts, fell subject to claims of ownership.[20]

As promotional and commercial interests capitalized on the homespun aura of organic quilting tradition, they were fashioning a synthetic equivalent in its place. Quilters were not only acquiring patterns and instructions from new sources, but they were also becoming consumers for products that modified homemade aspects of the craft and for changing aesthetic trends. Sears and its competitors offered quilters many degrees of participation in this consumership. While more self-sufficient quilters might purchase only a pattern, others could buy complete kits with precut pieces, which eliminated choices about fabric and the cloth recycling so often cited as a rationale for Depression quilting. For some needleworkers, piecing, and even quilting, by machine was a labor-saving temptation. A host of products provided shortcuts in technique, like the special pastes, iron-on transfers, perforated stencils, and wash-out pencils that simplified layout.

Popular culture also asserted pressure to modernize quilting tastes. As much as they evoked positive old-fashioned values, most authentic folk patchworks were notably out of step with the emergent design principles of the 1930s. Bridging this gap and "raising standards" in quilting was a priority of the aesthetic arbiters of the quilt revival. This circle, as evidenced by the panel of judges for the Century of Progress contest, was made up not of quilters, but of designers, collectors, home economists, and art authorities.[21] Quilt researchers have yet to fully document the influence of figures like Nashville's Anne Orr, needlework editor for *Good Housekeeping* and designer whose patterns were widely copied.

The intervention of these trendsetters in traditional quilting no doubt paralleled that of Appalachian craft industry organizers who, as outsiders to folk culture, worked to reform folk crafts according to their own artistic conceptions.[22] The Depression seemed to have inspired such dabbling with the folk heritage; literary creators of so-called "fakelore," for instance, were at the same time concocting fictional characters like Paul Bunyan and successfully passing them off as genuine folk heroes.[23]

Quilt designers introduced a full palette of pastel colors, art nouveau stylings, elaborately shaped borders, and floral and Dutch-girl appliqués often incongruously labeled "colonial." The dreamlike and sometimes luxuriant visual qualities of such designs contrasted sharply with the reality of hard times, making them akin to the escapist fare that the film industry served Depression audiences through lavish Busby Berkeley production numbers, optimistic rags-to-riches plots, and comedic treatments of despair.[24]

The appearance and symbolism of Depression quilts have tended to encourage us to look back at the 1930s in much the same distorted way that people then idealized colonial times. Quiltmaking exemplified domestic resolve to enlist skills of the past to cope with the crisis of the Depression. However attractive that idea was—and variations of it still are—it could not actually bring the past back into being. By the 1930s America had set a fundamentally modern course, and cultural expressions like quilting inevitably incorporated elements of both the old and the new. Between these extremes, the identities and meanings of specific Depression quilts are as individualized as the stitches that hold them together.

—Robert Cogswell
Director of Folk Arts
Tennessee Arts Commission

NOTES

1. Robert S. McElvaine, *The Great Depression: America, 1929–1941* (New York: Times Books, 1984), 7–12.

2. Daniel J. Boorstin, *The Americans: The Democratic Experience* (New York: Vintage Books, 1974), 89–136.

3. Henry Glassie, "Folk Art," in Richard M. Dorson, ed., *Folklore and Folklife: An Introduction* (Chicago: University of Chicago Press, 1972), 254–58.

4. Susan Prendergast Schoelwer, "Curious Relics and Quaint Scenes: The Colonial Revival at Chicago's Great Fair," in Alan Axelrod, ed., *The Colonial Revival in America* (New York: W. W. Norton, 1985), 184–216.

5. See McElvaine, 268–75; Susan Dwyer-Schick, "The Development of Folklore and Folklife Research in the Federal Writers' Project," *Keystone Folklore Quarterly* 29 (1975): 5–31; William Francis McDonald, *Federal Relief Administration and the Arts* (Columbus: Ohio State University Press, 1969); and E. O. Christensen, *The Index of American Design* (New York: MacMillan, 1950).

6. Louise Edelman, telephone interview with author, September 24, 1989. Mrs. Edelman first related her mother's experience to the author in 1982.

7. William G. Frost, "Our Contemporary Ancestors in the Southern Mountains," *Atlantic Monthly*, March 1899, 311–319.

8. Carrie A. Hall and Rose G. Kretsinger, *The Romance of the Patchwork Quilt in America* (New York: Bonanza, 1935), 16.

9. John C. Campbell, *The Southern Highlander and His Homeland*, rev. ed. (Lexington: University Press of Kentucky, 1969); and Allen H. Eaton, *Handicrafts of the Southern Highlands* (New York: Dover, 1973).

10. Cuesta Benberry, "Quilt Cottage Industries: A Chronicle," in Sally Garoutte, ed., *Uncoverings 1986*, vol. 7 (Mill Valley, California: American Quilt Study Group, 1986), 83–100.

11. Bill C. Malone, *Country Music, U.S.A.* (Austin: University of Texas Press, 1986), 3–78.

12. Cuesta Benberry, "A Record of National Quilt Contests," *Quilter's Newsletter Magazine*, 213, 28–30, 54; Barbara Brackman, "Quilts at Chicago's World's Fairs," in Sally Garoutte, ed., *Uncoverings 1981*, vol. 2 (Mill Valley, California: American Quilt Study Group, 1981), 63–76; and Barbara Brackman, "Looking Back at the Great Quilt Contest," *Quilter's Newsletter Magazine* 156, 22–24.

13. Guthrie T. Meade, "Fiddles and Fords," *Journal of Country Music* 12, no. 3 (1989): 37–45.

14. Brackman, "Looking Back at the Great Quilt Contest," 22.

15. F. W. Woolsey, "Jug Band," *Louisville Courier-Journal Magazine*, June 8, 1980, 10–12.

16. Malone, 174.

17. Ibid., 321.

18. Brackman, "Quilts at Chicago's World's Fairs," 70–71.

19. Ibid., 70; and Cuesta Benberry, "The Saga of One Quilt Pattern," *Nimble Needle Treasures* (Fall 1973), 15.

20. See, for example, G. Legman, "Who Owns Folklore?" *Western Folklore* 21 (1962): 1–12; and Norm Cohen, "Robert W. Gordon and the Second Wreck of 'Old 97,'" *Journal of American Folklore* 87 (1974): 12–38.

21. Brackman, "Quilts at Chicago's World's Fairs," 70.

22. David E. Whisnant, *All That Is Native and Fine: The Politics of Culture in an American Region* (Chapel Hill: University of North Carolina Press, 1983).

23. Richard M. Dorson, "Fakelore," in *American Folklore and the Historian* (Chicago: University of Chicago Press, 1971), 3–14, and "Paul Bunyan in the News," in *Folklore and Fakelore: Essays Toward a Discipline of Folk Studies* (Cambridge: Harvard University Press, 1976), 291–336.

24. Andrew Bergman, *We're in the Money: Depression America and Its Films* (New York: New York University Press, 1971).

SOFT COVERS

FOR

HARD TIMES

THE QUILT REVIVAL

The story of quiltmaking in the Great Depression begins with the Colonial Revival of the 1920s. As urban America roared through that decade, fueled by an interest in the nation's "colonial" past, the modern woman began to bring out her family heirloom quilts. If they were badly frayed, she copied them, using twentieth-century fabrics. If the cedar chest was bare, she made her own quilt or even purchased professionally made quilts to match her Early American furnishings.

In the rural areas, women had not stopped making quilts for warmth and comfort. Both urban and rural quiltmakers adopted new pieced and appliqué patterns and labor-saving innovations promoted nationally by large and small merchandising companies.

The companies capitalized on the "colonial" fad, but they incorrectly linked "colonial" and "old-fashioned" to pre-Victorian nineteenth-century styles rather than to eighteenth-century colonial styles. For quilts, that meant cotton pieced and appliqué designs were "in" and crazy quilts were "out."

The patriotic and nationalistic overtone of the term *colonial* did not hurt sales of products linked to the Colonial Revival. In 1915 Marie Webster, in *Quilts, Their Story and How to Make Them,* equated the quiltmaking tradition with high patriotic ideals. "Their construction . . . is steadily increasing in popularity. This should be a source of much satisfaction to all patriotic Americans who believe that the true source of our nation's strength lies in keeping the family hearth flame bright."[1]

Family, a hearth fire, and patriotic zeal were at the heart of the Colonial Revival. These symbols represent the spare, but noble, life, a life romanticized by a prosperous, secure society safely tucked in its steam-heated homes. The Colonial Revival of the 1920s stimulated antique collecting, the establishment of historic homes as museums, and even the

1. Detail of Basket and Blossom (See illustration 14).

reconstruction of historic Williamsburg, Virginia. Early American reproductions soon began replacing Victorian-style furnishings in the urban homes of middle- and upper-class families.

Since quilts fit the romanticized image of a colonial setting, the public was eager to complement their Early American bedroom furniture with quilts. Professionally made quilts became available through mail order houses, but many companies also sold quilt patterns. Some reprinted old patterns, but quilt designers knew that the modern woman would find patterns updated in modern colors and styles more appealing. This led to significant changes in the traditional design elements of the quilt.

Mid-nineteenth-century appliqué quilts have always been the most prized by makers' descendants and quilt collectors. Flowers made up in solid and calico-print fabrics were the preferred motifs. Most appliqué quilts of the mid-nineteenth century, especially in Tennessee, were not arranged around a central medallion, that is, a large central motif framed by multiple borders of pieced or appliqué designs. Instead, equal-sized block units made up nineteenth-century appliqué quilts. Some had as few as four large block units (See illustration 10). The field, or background fabric,

was usually white; and the appliqué motifs were pink, yellow, and light green or deep red, dark green, and yellow. The edges of the quilt were almost always straight.

Twentieth-century quilt designers such as Marie Webster, Rose Kretsinger, and Anne Orr favored the appliqué style, but they adapted certain elements to the 1920s decorating styles. Floral motifs remained popular in Colonial Revival quilts. Quilt designers maintained the use of solid colored fabric for the appliqué and lighter colored fabric for the background, but they substituted soft pastel colors for traditional nineteenth-century color combinations. The central medallion gained acceptance as an appliqué arrangement of the 1920s and 1930s, and a scalloped edge on a quilt often replaced straight edges (See illustration 2).

In 1911 and 1912 in *Ladies Home Journal,* Marie Webster presented eight appliqué quilts in full-color photographs. In them airy, dreamlike floral appliqué designs seem to float above the soft surface. Gone are the red, green, and yellow home-dyed hues of nineteenth-century quilts; instead, pale green, pink, blue, and yellow hues intertwine. Her quilts with scalloped edges and a central focus are designed to fit the bed.

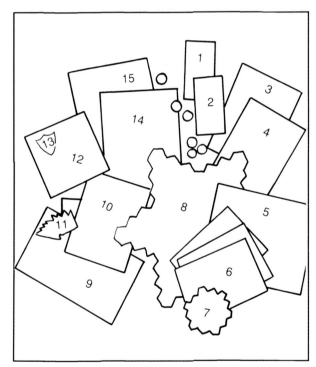

1. Kit with instructions and materials for making a yo-yo pillow; 2. completed yo-yo's ready for assembly; 3. quilt catalog (post 1930s); 4. quilt catalog (1940s); 5. Laura Wheeler instruction sheet for a quilt; 6. Ruby McKim quilt catalogs; 7. Grandmother's Flower Garden quilt block; 8. Grandmother's Flower Garden quilt block; 9. package of Grandmother's Perforated Quilting Patterns; 10. Needlecraft Supply Company mail order offer for pre-cut pieces for Broken Star quilt; 11. sample swatches of fabric offered for Broken Star quilt; 12. Fan quilt block made from a cloth kit of pre-cut and sorted pieces; 13. needle folder; 14. *Needlecraft Magazine* (September 1928); and 15. *Needlecraft Magazine* (December 1929).

(*Objects are from the collections of the Huff Family, Barbara Halgowich, and the author. Still life arranged by Sue Jenkins and Joyce Gralak.*)

2. WREATH OF ROSES

Maker: Pauline Clarke Hall.
Dickson, Dickson County, Tennessee, 1932.

Lender: Becky Salmon, granddaughter.

Appliqué: 82″ x 90½″; cotton: white and solid medium green, pink, rose, and yellow; fine white cotton back; pink bias binding; cotton batting; quilted in ⅝″ parallel lines in background and in floral motifs in center of wreaths and between blocks. Quilting thread is white.

This twentieth-century quilt has the sculpted edge and soft colors of typical Colonial Revival quilts. Marie Webster, a nationally known quilt designer, offered this pattern in the 1920s, but in an advertisement in *House Beautiful Magazine* in October 1932 she announced reduced prices on this quilt and others. Stamped quilt tops cost $8.00 to $12.00. Basted quilts cost $25.00 to $38.50. Her mail order company, Practical Patchwork Company in Marion, Indiana, also offered fine quilting services.

3. Detail of Wreath of Roses.

4. Pauline Clarke Hall and her husband, Frank S. Hall, at New York World's Fair, 1939.

Pauline Clarke Hall (1894–1984)

The daughter of a teacher in Clarksville, Tennessee, in 1913 Pauline Clarke married Frank S. Hall, son of a banker and builder of railroads. Frank S. Hall set up a legal practice in Dickson, Tennessee, in 1917 and was elected to the Tennessee State Legislature in 1919. In 1923 he became Speaker of the Tennessee House of Representatives, and in 1929 he was elected to the Tennessee State Senate. He served in various government capacities through 1945.

In 1932 Pauline Hall was overseeing the construction of a new family home in Dickson while her husband was working in

Although the Basket of Flowers (See illustration 6) designer is unknown, the quilt exemplifies the innovations of early twentieth-century quilt designs. This appliqué quilt in solid pastel colors has a bountiful central medallion, vine borders, and scalloped edges. Technology may have played a role in the change in quilt styles. An improved textile industry provided a broad range of pastel-colored fabric not available to nineteenth-century women, and machine-made bias tape introduced in the early twentieth century enabled easy binding of scalloped edges.

The Basket of Flowers shows the popularity of embroidery in the 1920s. The stylized basket with flowing ribbon was not a popular motif in appliqué quilts in the 1800s, but it was a popular embroidery design for handkerchiefs and other linens in the early 1900s. It is not surprising then to see embroidery designs incorporated in commercial quilt patterns.

5. Detail of Basket of Flowers.

Nashville. That year she apparently made the Wreath of Roses quilt; it was the only fancy quilt she is known to have made. Her favorite saying was, "When you do something and you do it well, then you can't top it."

6. BASKET OF FLOWERS

Ida Virginia Strong Reed (1869–1938)

Maker: Ida Virginia Strong Reed.
  Columbia, Maury County, Tennessee, 1925–1938.

Leaner: Virginia Reed Tobias, granddaughter.

Appliqué 82″ x 93½″; cotton: assorted pastels and white; white cotton back; green bias binding; cotton batting; quilting includes wreaths and 1½-inch diamonds in background. Quilted plume designs in borders. Embroidery accents on flowers and butterflies.

Typical of Colonial Revival quilts, this quilt has a central focus, scalloped edges and an exuberant display of flowers in a basket bedecked with a flowing ribbon. Although the printed pattern has not been found, this quilt probably was made with instructions on cutting and placement of the appliqué pieces.

Ida Reed, who grew up in a cotton mill worker's family and married a mill worker, had a hard life. In 1891 she and her husband, James Reed, were able to build a house across from the factory cottages; and he had a new job as a railroad electrician. He died after an accident in 1917, leaving Ida with three children to raise.

Ida is remembered as a perfect grandmother. In the 1930s her grandchildren stayed with her for two weeks when their parents went to the Chicago World's Fair. Ida entertained her grandchildren with tea parties and picnics. She always wore old-fashioned bonnets, but she was a modern woman and very education-minded.

Ida made hooked rugs of strips of rayon brought home by her son from the DuPont plant where he worked, and she made many utility string quilts. Her best needlework skills were saved for the Basket of Flowers appliqué quilt that she gave to her son.

7. WASHINGTON'S PLUME

Washington's Plume (See illustration 7) is such a precise reproduction of a nineteenth-century appliqué quilt pattern that one might mistake it for an older quilt. The maker copied a family heirloom quilt and kept the traditional color combination of red and green with highlights of yellow and pink. Notice also that this quiltmaker has maintained the straight edges of earlier quilts. The staggered block arrangement is an innovation that gives the quilt a balanced effect.

Maker: Beulah Watkins Marshall.
  Dandridge, Jefferson County, Tennessee, 1931–1935.

Lender: Mable Marshall Westbrooks, daughter.

Appliqué: 69″ x 71″; cotton: red, pink, yellow, and green solids on white background; white cotton back; red binding on the straight; cotton batting; quilted garlands in plain areas with parallel lines ½″ apart in background; quilted by the piece in appliqué; quilting thread matches color of appliqué pieces.

The maker copied a family heirloom quilt called Princess Feather and renamed it in honor of George Washington, whose two hundredth birthday was celebrated widely in 1932. The maker had kept the color combination and the straight edges typical of nineteenth-century Tennessee quilts.

[8]

8. Detail of Washington's Plume.

10. Plume and Rose appliqué quilt, dated 1869. Maker Frances Carter Shipe of Clinton, Tennessee.

9. Beulah Watkins Marshall with husband, Rev. T. O. Marshall, a Methodist minister for five churches in and around Dandridge, Tennessee.

Beulah Watkins Marshall (1899–1975)

Beulah Watkins married Rev. T. O. Marshall in 1923. To their union were born two children, Mable and Carolyn. From 1931 to 1935, Rev. Marshall was minister of a circuit of five Methodist churches around Dandridge, Tennessee. He took his salary there in produce instead of cash, and the church furnished the house; the family was warm and well-fed. When Rev. Marshall performed a wedding, he was given a wedding fee, which he handed over immediately to his wife to buy special fabric for her craft work or whatever.

Beulah made many quilts in traditional patterns such as Bear Paw and Trip Around the World. She swapped patterns with neighbors and probably got some of the patterns from *Farm Home Journal* or a local newspaper.

Besides quilting, she did knitting, crocheting, tatting, crewel work, and straight embroidery.

11. Souvenir of bicentennial celebration of the birth of George Washington. The celebration increased interest in the country's colonial past. Collection of the author.

Rose Kretsinger, an artist and quilt historian, adapted an appliqué quilt design of a nineteenth-century quilt. Her design was in rose, light pink, and green. The updated quilt, called Oriental Poppy, appeared in *The Romance of the Patchwork Quilt in America,* which Kretsinger wrote with Carrie Hall.[2] The quilt pattern was also sold nationally through *Farm Journal and Farmer's Wife.*

When Bernice Schultz Mackey made the Oriental Poppy (See illustration 13) from the Kretsinger pattern, she used red rather than the suggested pink. Her choice was closer to the traditional appliqué color combination than Kretsinger's. Bernice purchased the appliqué fabric but used bleached feedsacks for the background. The lining of her quilt was also bleached feedsacks.

The quiltmaking frenzy continued unabated long after the stock market crash of 1929. A look at the advertising section of any women's magazine of the 1930s is proof of the renaissance of quiltmaking and of new ready-made aspects of quilt supply marketing. The January 1933 issue of *Needlecraft* had the following offers: "500 quilt patches $1.00 cut to size" from John C. Michael Company of Chicago, Illinois; "Rainbow Quilt Blocks $1.00 per dozen," "Quilt pieces 25 cents," from C. O. Olson of Grandy, Minnesota; *Ladies Art Company Catalog* for 25 cents; and "Fibre patterns for cutting patches" from W. L. M. Clark.

Large and small entrepreneurs saw the money-making opportunities in quiltmaking and introduced new time-saving products to encourage thousands of reluctant women to "make a quilt." For years traditional quiltmakers had followed the same time-consuming tasks: making patterns, marking and cutting fabric, and sewing pieces together. The actual quilting required more pattern making and marking.

12. Bernice Schultz Mackey with her Oriental Poppy quilt, 1985. Photo courtesy of the Tennessee Department of Tourism.

Bernice Schultz Mackey (b. 1916)

Bernice Schultz Mackey, known as "Tootsie," was the only living quiltmaker featured in *The Quilts of Tennessee* exhibit and book. Her interview in the book's chapter entitled "Quilting Lessons from Childhood" is evidence of the importance of recording oral histories of living quiltmakers.

Tootsie began to quilt when she was eight years old. When she was twelve, she began the Oriental Poppy. For the appliqué, she pinned down the pieces and stitched around them using a whip stitch. She quilted each block separately on her lap. She pieced the triangle set and attached it to the squares. She said it did not take so long to make. It was her favorite quilt.

She still does a lot of sewing. "I get up in the morning and never stop." She has made luncheon sets, satin pillow cases, and at least one hundred nightgowns. She feels sewing is her gift from God. She has never sold any, saying, "it is more fun to make them and give them away."

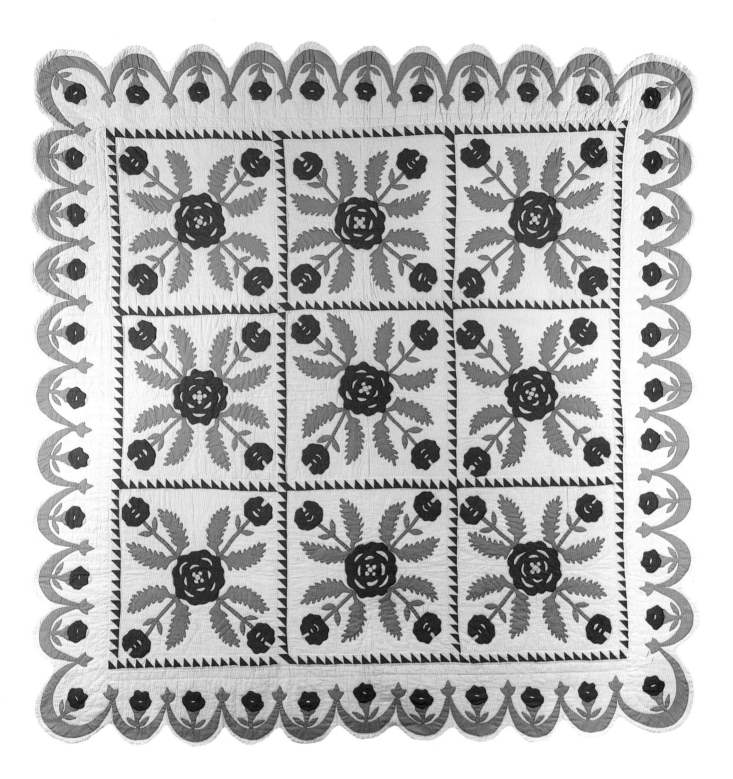

13. ORIENTAL POPPY

Maker: Bernice Schultz Mackey.
   Huntland, Franklin County, Tennessee.

Lender: Bernice "Tootsie" Schultz Mackey.

Pieced and appliqué: 86″ x 88″; cotton: red, green, and pink solids
   and muslin; feedsack back; knife edge; cotton batting; quilted by
   the piece and around appliqué motifs in white thread.

Tootsie ordered the ten-cent Oriental Poppy pattern. Rather than
transfer the quilt pieces onto tracing paper, she cut them out of the
printed sheet. The quilt, designed by Rose Kretsinger of Emporia,
Kansas, in the 1920s, is in *The Romance of the Patchwork Quilt in
America* by Carrie Hall and Rose Kretsinger. This so-called Colonial
Revival pattern is an adaptation of a quilt made in the late 1800s.

In the nineteenth century, before printed patterns were widely circulated, quiltmakers had their own method of saving patterns. After seeing a quilt, or perhaps receiving a sketch from a friend, the quilter worked the design in fabric to make a sample block. It served as a record of the pattern and was sometimes joined with other such blocks to make a sample quilt.

In the early 1900s, the term *quilt pattern* was expanded. It was still the illustration used to assemble the block, but it could be a simple hand-drawn picture on lined paper or a commercially printed pattern complete with layout instructions. Similar to a dress pattern, the commercial quilt pattern came in a large envelope with actual size pieces printed on a large sheet of paper. When traced and then transferred to heavy paper, the pattern pieces became templates used for drawing the shapes on the fabric. The pattern envelope also included detailed instructions on construction of the quilt top, color choice, and finishing.

Pattern making and fabric marking were easier with the transfer pattern introduced in the early 1900s. Quiltmakers no longer had to trace pattern pieces and mark lines for cutting and sewing. A quilter simply passed a hot iron over the transfer pattern, leaving an ink design on the fabric.

Transfer patterns were especially helpful in making appliqué quilts. When quiltmakers transferred the shapes directly to the cloth, they also got the stitching and cutting lines. Some women transferred the pattern shapes to heavy paper to make reusable cutting templates. Appliqué placement guides transferred to the white cloth also allowed for faster, more precise construction.

In March 1933, the *Knoxville News-Sentinel* offered "The Wonder Package" to its women readers. The new process was a cold transfer process. "No more hot irons—no more waste!" The package had twelve sheets, each twenty-four by thirty-six inches. These sheets were covered with more than eight hundred of the very latest designs of embroidery and full-size squares for appliqué and patchwork quilts. With the Wonder Process, the quilter simply had to dampen the pattern on the reverse side, place the fabric under it, and rub the pattern firmly with the bowl of a tablespoon. "Instant, perfect transfers!" Best of all, according to the advertiser, the "cold process" allowed patterns to be used over and over again. Cost of the Wonder Package was one dollar if mailed, and eighty-eight cents if the person appeared in person at the *News-Sentinel* office.[3]

Like the construction of the quilt top, the quilting process required templates and fabric marking before the first stitch was taken. Many women reported that they marked the quilting lines by eye or followed the seam lines of the pieces, but if an intricate quilting design was to be "laid off," lead pencils or chalk were often used. Both had disadvantages. Lead did not always wash out, and chalk sometimes disappeared before quilting began.

Addie Lee Cope Butler Daniel (1902–1977)

In 1923 Addie Lee Cope married George Butler. Sixteen months later they both contracted typhoid fever, and he died in 1924. She lived with her parents, James and Susie Cope, on their 450-acre farm in Henry County, Tennessee, for many years. The Cope house was a place filled with quilts, quilting, lots of good food, and warm hospitality. In 1938 she married Jack Daniel.

Addie learned how to make quilts from her mother and grandmother. The women excelled in piecing. In a folder marked "patterns," daughter Emily Cox found several quilt patterns cut from newspapers, farm magazines, paper bags, and cardboard. There were no purchased patterns.

Besides quilt-piecing, Addie did embroidery, tatting, hairpin trimming, rug hooking, and sewing for her daughter. She became well-known for making clothes and booties for antique and reproduction dolls.

When Addie died, her daughter had a crochet needle put in her hand with a partially made Granny square. "Thinking back on that, it seems weird, but Mama just didn't look like herself without something in her hands."

Sears, Roebuck and Company offered perforated quilting patterns and stamping wax: "No more tiresome marking of quilts in the old-fashioned way."[4] The stamping outfit included a packet of stencils of traditional quilting patterns and a jar of black or yellow paste. The quilter simply placed the stencil on the quilt top and rubbed the paste lightly over it with a cotton ball dipped in gasoline. This left on the cloth a dotted line to follow when doing the quilting.

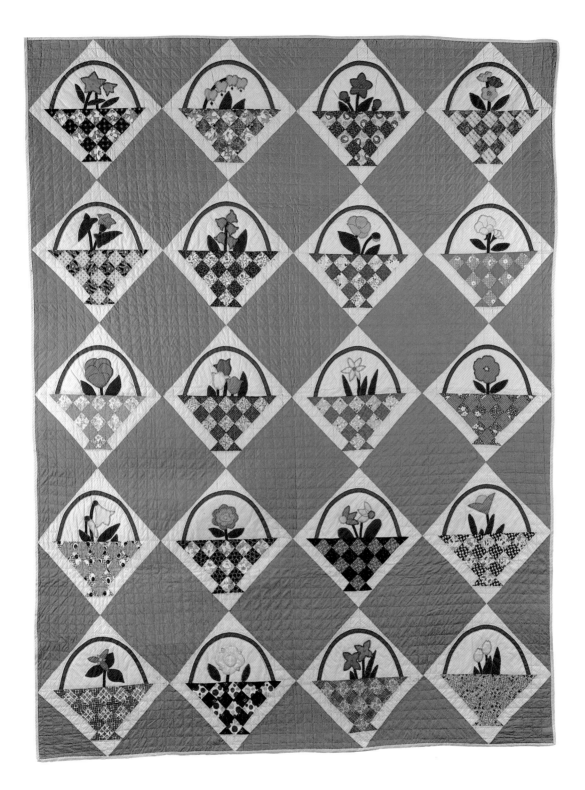

14. BASKET AND BLOSSOM

Maker: Addie Lee Cope Butler Daniel.
Henry County, Tennessee, 1930.

Lender: Emily Daniel Cox, daughter.

Pieced and appliqué: 62″ x 84″; cotton: white, blue, and various
  calico prints; white muslin back; pink bias binding; cotton
  batting; cross hatch quilting in lines 1¼ inches apart except
  behind flowers. Machine appliqué on basket handles and blanket
  stitch on floral appliqués.

Addie's mother and grandmother were great quilters. The shelves
on either side of the fireplace in the sitting room were full of bolts
of material. While most quiltmakers used scraps, all these women
had to do was open up the cupboards. The women also collected
printed quilt patterns. This quilt was probably made from a series
of blocks which appeared in a newspaper.

In 1933 Lena Davis of Vasper, Tennessee, enclosed a letter with squares she had stamped for Mrs. Murray of Mohawk, Tennessee:

> At last the squares are done and will soon be on their way to you. I hope I have not kept you waiting. . . . The broad cloth stamped very nicely. . . . These squares will have an awful odor of gasoline I'm sure, for I only finished them last night and they haven't been in the air long enough. My stamping outfit came from Idaho and I gave it to a friend of mine but I can still use it anytime I wish so tell Maggie Sue to send her material to me and I'll be glad to stamp one for her. . . . It won't be a particle of trouble.[5]

Lena Davis's cooperative spirit in sharing her new tool also reflects the thriftiness required by the hard times.

For women who were willing to pay the extra money, some patterns came as kits with the pattern pieces already stamped on the cloth. An appliqué Pansy quilt kit offered by *Needlecraft Magazine* for $3.49 included a bleached cotton sheet stamped with appliqué placements and quilting lines. Colored fabrics in the kit were stamped for the appliqué patches. The quiltmaker simply cut out the appliqué patch and applied it to its stamped location on the sheet.[6] This jokingly has been called "the paint by number" technique of quiltmaking.

Still other kits came with die-cut fabric pieces sorted by color. The quilter simply sewed the fabric pieces together, still a time-consuming job. In 1932 the Frederick Herrschner Company of Chicago offered a Double Wedding Ring quilt package for the special price of $3.95 that included sufficient pieces of die-cut materials to complete the quilt. It advertised, "All pieces are of fast color Chintz Prints and perfectly die-cut, making them easy to join together."[7]

For those lucky women unaffected by hard times, there was another opportunity to own a quilt. Many companies advertised ready-made quilts. The Ladies' Art Company offered to make whole quilts to order from any design in their catalog. Anne Orr offered professionally made quilts. In her January 1938 *Good Housekeeping* column, she wrote: "There is a woman in the South, with sixty mountain women working under her direction, who will do quilting."[8] However, the vast majority of American women lived on farms or had limited resources and made quilts the old-fashioned way.

Information about new printed quilt patterns circulated easily and rapidly. Newspapers were inexpensive, and shopping by mail order catalogs was common. Most rural women did not order patterns but copied them from newspapers and magazines. If a woman actually bought a pattern, it was usually passed from friend to friend.

The Huff sisters of Loudon County, Tennessee, were the exception. They ordered dozens of patterns from magazines, newspapers, and catalogs. More importantly, they saved these paper items which today serve as invaluable historical documents.

15. Ladies' Art Company of St. Louis, Missouri, sent the Four Tulips design card from which the Huff sisters made the cutting templates for their quilt pieces.

Mary Jane Huff (1879–1942) and her sister Linna Belle Huff (1881–1969) lived on a prosperous farm in Loudon County. Neither Huff sister married, but they quilted as if they had many children. The quilt revival of the early twentieth century greatly affected the type of quiltmaking they did.

Rachel Huff Wilson, their niece, who lived with them while she was growing up in the 1920s, has reported that her aunts were always busy with their hands. After lunch they would sit on the back porch and piece quilts. In the early 1900s Mary Jane Huff probably got pieces of cloth for her quilts at the dry goods store in Loudon where she worked. Mary Jane kept cows, reused feedsacks, knitted, crocheted, and made dresses for Rachel when she left to go to college.

After Mary Jane died in 1942, Linna Belle no longer quilted, but she kept their collection intact. Today their relatives treasure many quilts and three cardboard boxes containing quilt articles, quilt patterns, quilt catalogs, sample blocks, and unfinished quilt tops. Included in the Huff sisters' collection are quilt articles spanning the years from 1906 to 1933 clipped from *Southern Agriculturalist, Farm & Fireside, Needlecraft Magazine, Comfort, Woman's World, Modern Priscilla, Holland's: The Magazine of the South,* and

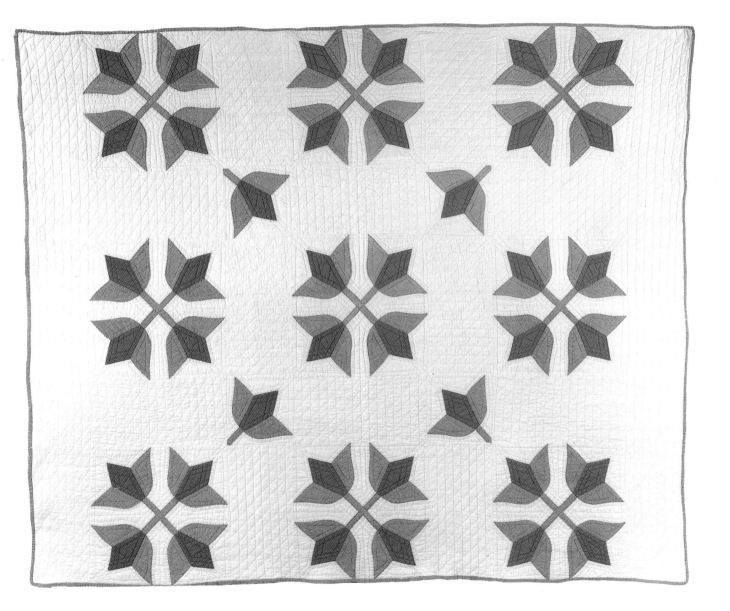

16. Mary Jane Huff.   **17.** Linna Belle Huff.

18. FOUR TULIPS

Maker: Mary Jane and Linna Belle Huff.
    Loudon, Loudon County, Tennessee, 1930.

Lender: Rachel Huff Wilson, niece.

Pieced: 64″ x 80″; cotton: handwoven small checked fabric and
    purple and white solid cotton batting; white back; handwoven
    small checked binding; quilted by the piece and in diamonds in
    plain blocks using white thread; cotton batting.

The Huff sisters ordered dozens of quilt catalogs and quilt patterns
from mail order companies in the Midwest. This pattern came from
the Ladies' Art Company in St. Louis, Missouri. They made their
own templates using the purchased patterns as guides. This block
arrangement creates a central focus which was becoming a popular
quilt style in the early twentieth century.

Delineator. The earlier magazines, such as *Woman's World,* published quilt blocks sent in by readers but did not sell patterns. The later magazines, such as *Southern Agriculturalist,* sold patterns for their illustrated quilts.

Some quilt articles were simply advertisements for mail order pattern companies, but that did not bother the Huff sisters. They paid twenty-five cents for a catalog of the Ladies' Art Company of St. Louis filled with hundreds of quilt patterns to order. A page clipped from the *Frederick Herrschner Fall and Winter 1932–1933* catalog printed in Chicago offered quilt kits for sale. Three *Patchwork Patterns* booklets by Ruby McKim, *Grandma Dexter Patchwork Designs Book,* and the *Sears Century of Progress in Quilt Making* had pattern pieces to trace; but they also served as advertising for the companies' other products and patterns.

Probably the most common source of quilt patterns during the 1930s in Tennessee was the local newspaper. Although the Huff sisters lived on a farm in the country, they were close enough to Knoxville to receive the *Knoxville Journal* on a regular basis. In 1933 a different Laura Wheeler needlecraft pattern appeared four times a week. The Huff sisters clipped seventy-seven different patterns, several of which had duplicates.

Laura Wheeler patterns were produced and syndicated by the Old Chelsea Station Needlecraft Service of New York. Readers sent ten cents or stamps (coins preferred) to a New York address requesting the pattern by number. The Huff sisters carefully clipped the illustration, the accompanying explanation, and the ordering information; and they ordered at least one pattern, number 486, Old Fashioned Nosegay.

Laura Wheeler patterns were popular because they were often for pieced quilts using scrap fabrics, a style of quilt popular in rural Tennessee. The Laura Wheeler patterns cost only ten cents, but readers could easily make quilts from the illustrated pattern that showed several blocks and gave the reader a good idea of the overall effect of the quilt. Also the three-inch square pattern presented on a grid made it easy to scale up pattern pieces (See illustration 24).

19. Detail of State Flower Quilt shows maker's deliberate change from passion flower to iris.

Rubye Nelson Seymour (1889–1954)

Rubye Nelson married Joseph Seymour, a successful doctor in Whiteville, Tennessee, where they raised five children. Her husband had a very successful medical practice, and he was able to buy the first car in the West Tennessee town. The community loved and revered him, but during the Great Depression he suffered financially as his patients were unable to pay for his service or the medicine he dispersed. He continued his practice, however, and often would accompany patients on the train to a Memphis hospital for further treatment or surgery.

In the late 1940s, the people of the town had a Dr. Seymour Appreciation Day. The two hundred people who came gave him an electric range trying to repay him in some way.

When the State Flower quilt was made in the 1930s, Rubye's children were grown. She enjoyed her large flower garden full of poppies and lilacs. In addition to quiltmaking and gardening, she sewed for her daughters and especially liked to add fine appliqué to their dresses.

20. STATE FLOWER QUILT

Maker: Rubye Nelson Seymour.
   Near Whiteville in Haywood County, Tennessee, 1933.

Lender: Allene Blalock, granddaughter.

Pieced and embroidered: 61″ x 77″; cotton: purple, pink and white
   solids; various colors of cotton embroidery thread; pink cotton
   back; purple bias binding; cotton batting; shell quilting in set
   and concentric fan quilting in blocks.

In the early 1930s quilt designer Ruby McKim's State Flower
patterns appeared weekly in newspapers throughout the United
States. Readers clipped the actual-size patterns and transferred them
to blocks of fabric using carbon paper. Mrs. Seymour made one
change in the pattern. She substituted an appliqué iris for the
Tennessee block in the McKim pattern because in 1933 the iris
became the state flower of Tennessee replacing the passion flower.

The straightforward approach of the writers of Laura Wheeler no doubt also appealed to Tennessee quiltmakers carrying on a tradition begun by their grandmothers. Accompanying pattern number 600, for example, is this statement: "When a quiltmaker chooses a pattern, she wants more than an economical and easy-to-make quilt. It must be attractive and one which she will always be proud to possess."[9] No short cuts are offered in these patterns, just complete, simple instructions and diagrams to help arrange blocks—all for ten cents.

In 1933 the *Chattanooga Times* and the *Nashville Banner* carried another nationally syndicated quilt column: Nancy Page. Written by Florence La Ganke, the column was a chatty account of the weekly Nancy Page Quilt Club meeting. Members could cut the pattern out of the newspaper for their scrapbook, but they had to send three cents and a self-addressed, stamped envelope for the actual-size pattern to make the blocks.

22. Jennie Lowry Hall and her husband Ben Calvin Hall on steps of their home near Vonore, Tennessee, 1950s.

21. The 1933 Laura Wheeler newspaper pattern Jennie Lowry Hall used to make her Swing in the Center quilt. Collection of Lois Hall.

23. 1930s quilting group near Vonore, Tennessee. Jennie Lowry Hall, maker of Swing in the Center quilt (See illustration 24), is first from left in back row.

24. SWING IN THE CENTER

Maker: Jennie Lowry Hall.
  Near Vonore, Monroe County, Tennessee, 1930s.

Lender: Lois Hall, daughter.

Pieced: 67″ x 87″; cotton: white and green solids, and printed
  chicken feed sacks; white cotton back; white bias binding; cotton
  batting; quilting is by the piece in white cotton thread.

The quilt is made from one of the Laura Wheeler designs which
appeared several times per week in newspapers throughout the
country. The *Knoxville Journal* carried the patterns in the early
1930s. The full pattern with instructions cost ten cents, but many
women simply clipped the illustrations to make their own templates
at a later time.

25. 1932 wrapper of Stearns and Foster's popular Mountain Mist batting includes old patterns renamed and adapted for the modern market. Collection of the author.

26. Eula and Buford Erwin stand at left of inmates and staff of the Women's State Prison near Nashville, 1933. Photo courtesy of Mary Dunn and Sallie Will Harris, daughters of Eula and Buford Erwin.

The Nancy Page column often included a two-inch-square illustration of a quilt pattern submitted by a reader. The Bull's Eye pattern featured on May 9, 1933, in the *Nashville Banner* was submitted by a woman in Granite City, Illinois (See illustration 27). The prisoners at the Women's State Prison in Nashville made the Bull's Eye quilt about that time (See illustration 28).

Nancy Page also offered a weekly series of quilt blocks, some in actual sizes. In 1933 the Old Almanac Quilt series was underway. With the pattern for Virgo cut from the paper, the Nancy Page Club members were instructed to take out their six-inch-square of transfer or carbon paper and lay it over a six and one-half inch-square of blue cloth to transfer the name *Virgo* and the dates to the cloth. Then they should transfer the zodiac design to cardboard. Embroidery of the name and dates covered up the transfer lines. The zodiac design on cardboard was used to cut out the design in a colorful print fabric.

The Nancy Page column often sounded as if it was written for a group of young girls inexperienced in needlework. In the Virgo column, for instance, readers were encouraged to use "stitches heavy enough to give solidity to the words, otherwise they looked like the spidery writing of an old, old person."[10] Other times, it was written for the busy homemaker and even provides recipes for a perfect luncheon.

The Memphis *Commercial Appeal* carried yet another syndicated quilt column published by the Needleart Company of Chicago, Illinois. The illustration of the quilt block that appeared as often as five times per week varied in size from day to day. Some days it was the size of Laura Wheeler patterns, but on other days it was as small as Nancy Page's patterns sent in by readers. The column advertised the *The Colonial Quilt Book* and explained it had "32 pages showing over 200 of the most popular designs in lovely color combinations." The cost of the booklet was only twenty-five cents, but the quilter still had to order a full-size pattern separately.

The Needleart Company of Chicago was known for its central medallion star quilts designed by H. Ver Mehren, owner of the company. A quilt made from the Star of France pattern was exhibited at the Sears National Quilt Exhibition at the Chicago World's Fair in 1933. Several exact duplicates of the quilt exist because the pattern was sold as a cloth kit. The advertisement proclaims:

All of the material for making the top of this beautiful quilt can be had stamped with lines to cut on and with stamped lines to sew on." Prices varied according to one's choice of fabric but the most expensive was in sateen for $5.95. If you wanted to make the quilt yourself, a complete cutting guide, perforated quilting patterns, stamping powder, and a color chart cost one dollar.[11]

Where did these companies get quilt patterns? Writers of the Nancy Page and Needleart columns freely admitted their patterns were submitted by readers. Needleart Company encouraged readers to send them descriptions of their family heirlooms so that patterns could be made up. The Ladies' Art Company also collected quilt patterns from a wide variety of sources. Companies usually assigned new names to their updated patterns, which led to the loss of some regional names.

The Stearns and Foster Company of Cincinnati, for example, changed the names of patterns they chose for the wrapper of their Mountain Mist cotton batting. The quilt patterns on the 1932 wrapper were borrowed from a variety of sources. The pattern identified by the company as New York Beauty was called Rocky Mountain Road or Crown of Thorns in the nineteenth century. Because of the popularity of the Mountain Mist pattern, the older names were forgotten. No southern quiltmaker would have made a quilt with a Yankee name during the Reconstruction period. Today some people in the South call their nineteenth-century Crown of Thorns quilts News York Beauty (See illustration 30).

Stearns and Foster also featured patterns designed by well-known quilt designers. Whether or not the designers

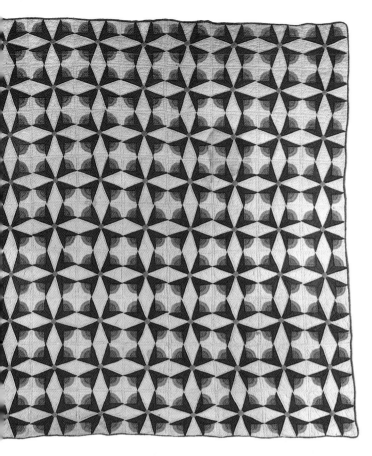

28. BULL'S EYE

Makers: Inmates at the Women's Prison.
West Nashville, Davidson County, Tennessee, circa. 1933.

Lender: Kay Hardy, niece of Eula Erwin, matron at the prison.

Pieced: 71″ x 74″; cotton: white, green, yellow, and pink solids; white cotton back; green bias binding; cotton batting, quilted by the piece.

When the Bull's Eye quilt pattern appeared in the May 9, 1933, *Nashville Banner*, Eula Erwin might have clipped it out. She and her husband, Buford, were caretakers of the women's prison at the time. She encouraged the women to quilt to occupy their time. They also had flower gardens, vegetable gardens, laundry rooms, dining and cooking areas to work in as well as a small infirmary. Mrs. Erwin bought the materials for the quilts and sometimes used scraps from worn-out inmates' uniforms. About fifty women were at the prison. Some had killed their husbands, one had embezzled money, but most had not committed violent crimes.

27. The May 9, 1933, Nancy Page quilt column in the *Nashville Banner* included the Bull's Eye pattern submitted by a reader in Granite City, Illinois.

29. Detail of Bull's Eye.

30. NEW YORK BEAUTY

Maker: Possibly Sarah Moore.
Meigs County, Tennessee, circa 1935.

Lender: Clara Carmichael.

Pieced: 80″ x 85½″; cotton: white, pink, and yellow solids, and assorted calico prints; set and borders are green and white; white percale back; cotton batting; edge turned back to front; quilted by the piece except in the white centers and the sashing where leaves and flowers are quilted. Quilting thread is white.

This pattern was commonly called Rocky Mountain Road or Crown of Thorns in the 1800s in the South. When the pattern was printed commercially in the twentieth century, it was renamed New York Beauty. The quilt's pastel colors and lively calico prints are typical of Depression-era quilts. Sarah Moore quilted for the family of Lizzie Lee Hornsby. Sarah Moore's Schoolhouse quilt was featured in *The Quilts of Tennessee: Images of Domestic Life Prior to 1930*.

31. SUNFLOWER

Maker: Belle Marlin Gilmore.
  Murfreesboro, Rutherford County, Tennessee, 1939–1940.

Lender: Jeanne Gilmore Webb, daughter.

Appliqué: 73″ x 86½″; cotton: muslin with gold, brown, and green
  solids; muslin back; cotton batting; gold bias binding; quilted in
  sunflower and leaf motifs in background and ½-inch diamonds,
  circles and one-inch diamonds in border. Quilting thread is white.

Marie Webster's appliqué Sunflower quilt was published in January
1912 in *Ladies' Home Journal,* and then again in 1926 in her book
Quilts Their Story and How to Make Them. Stearns and Foster
adapted the Sunflower design and included it on their Mountain
Mist cotton batting wrapper as early as 1932.

32. Detail of Sunflower.

33. Belle Marlin Gilmore
with husband Thomas, 1940.

Belle Marlin Gilmore (1888–1956)

Belle, her three sisters, and her mother were all accomplished
needleworkers. They had attended Soule College, a girls' boarding
school in Murfreesboro, Tennessee, where needlework was taught,
but not to the exclusion of languages, mathematics, science, and
humanities. With her sisters and mother, Belle shared needlework
patterns and ideas from such periodicals as *Delineator, Ladies' Home
Journal, Needlecraft, Farm Journal, Progressive Farmer, Southern
Agriculturist* and *Good Housekeeping.*

According to her daughter, Jeanne, Belle tried most types of
handwork except spinning and weaving. She sewed most garments
needed by the family and remodeled garments during the
Depression. Also, tablecloths, napkins, pillow cases, sheets, hand
towels, doilies, and dresser scarves were embellished with drawn
work, cutwork, counted stitch, and embroidered monograms and/or
floral designs. She made the Sunflower quilt from a pattern offered
on a Mountain Mist batting wrapper. Her husband, Tom Gilmore,
marked the appliqué pieces and the quilting design with a hard
lead pencil. The quilt was given to Jeanne as a graduation gift in
1941.

34. Detail of Dresden Plate.

were paid for the use of their patterns is not known, and the designers were never credited on the wrapper illustrations. The appliqué Sunflower was one of several patterns adapted from a Marie Webster design that first appeared in full color in *Ladies Home Journal* in 1911 and 1912. Webster also included the pattern in her popular book *Quilts: Their Story and How to Make Them* published in 1915. Belle Marlin Gilmore made the Sunflower quilt from a Stearns and Foster pattern in 1939 (See illustration 31).

Of the thousands of quilt patterns distributed throughout the country, a few became so widely accepted that they have become classic quilt designs. Grandmother's Flower Garden, Dresden Plate (See illustration 35), Double Wedding Ring, and Sunbonnet Sue in soft pastel decorator colors were produced by hundreds of thousands of women in all parts of the United States during the quilt revival. These quilts sharply contrast with their nineteenth-century precursors and the hard times of the Great Depression. What caused the change in look and construction to be so widely accepted? Was it the romanticized Colonial Revival, or was it a healthy textile industry churning our inexpensive cotton in pastel shades? No doubt both contributed; but credit also must go to the mass marketing strategies that by the 1930s had already caused homogenization of culture, ideas, and even quilt design.

35. DRESDEN PLATE

Maker: Viola Sanders Webb.
   Keltonburg Community, DeKalb County, Tennessee, 1935.

Lender: Frances Whittemore, niece.

Pieced and appliqué: 89″ x 89″; cotton: assorted calico prints and muslin; white cotton back; white bias binding; cotton batting; diamond quilting in background and by the piece in blocks and border in white thread.

This version of the popular Dresden Plate pattern appeared in *Successful Farming* magazine and the *Home Art Studios* mail order catalog. Viola Webb made the quilt for one of her nieces whose mother purchased the pattern and the fabric for the quilt. Viola usually made quilts with what she had on hand. The consistent placement of the red print fabric gives the quilt a balanced look sometimes missing in scrap quilts. (See pages 69–75 for Viola Webb's story.)

[23]

REFINING THE TRADITION

Anne Champe Orr, 1875–1946

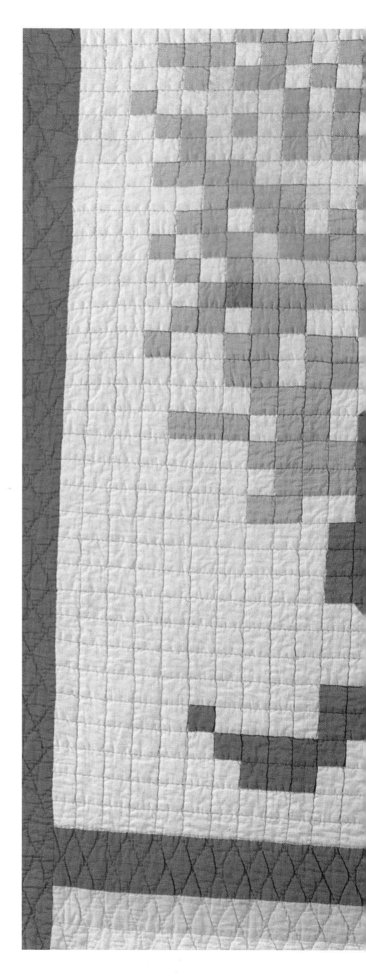

Anne Champe Orr is Tennessee's own nationally known quilt designer. Like quilt designers Marie Webster of Indiana, Ruby McKim of Missouri, and Rose Kretsinger of Kansas, who came to national prominence in the 1920s, Anne Orr hoped to raise quilt-making to an art. Her audience was made up of the modern women who wanted to decorate their homes with Early American furnishings. Anne Orr was best known as a designer of needlework, especially counted cross-stitch. But, as interest in quiltmaking increased, she added quilt patterns to her mail order offerings. By 1932 she was so well known as a quilt designer that she was asked to judge the first national quilt contest at Storrowton Village in Springfield, Massachusetts, in the summer of 1932 and the Sears, Roebuck Quilt Contest in the summer of 1933. She promoted her Nashville mail order pattern service through her monthly column in *Good Housekeeping* and was considered a highly successful businesswoman in Nashville.

Following her death in 1946, her daughters continued to operate her business for a short while; but it eventually closed. Although her needlework patterns are still sold nationally, her quilt patterns are not. Few Anne Orr quilt patterns are indexed in encyclopedias of quilt blocks; consequently, her name is not as well known as it once was.

To honor Anne Orr's contributions to the twentieth-century quilting renaissance, the Continental Quilting Congress inducted her into the Quilter's Hall of Fame in 1980. The proclamation pointed out that "she dedicated her career to bringing needleworkers good, appropriate design, and in the process, gave many craftswomen creative employment."[1]

Anne Orr began her writing career in 1913 with *Southern Woman's Magazine* published in Nashville. For the first two years her column included a variety of cross-stitch embroidery designs as well as tatting, filet crochet, and knitting patterns. Her favorite motifs were baskets with bows, herons, peacocks, swans, butterflies, Dutch windmills, and sailboats.

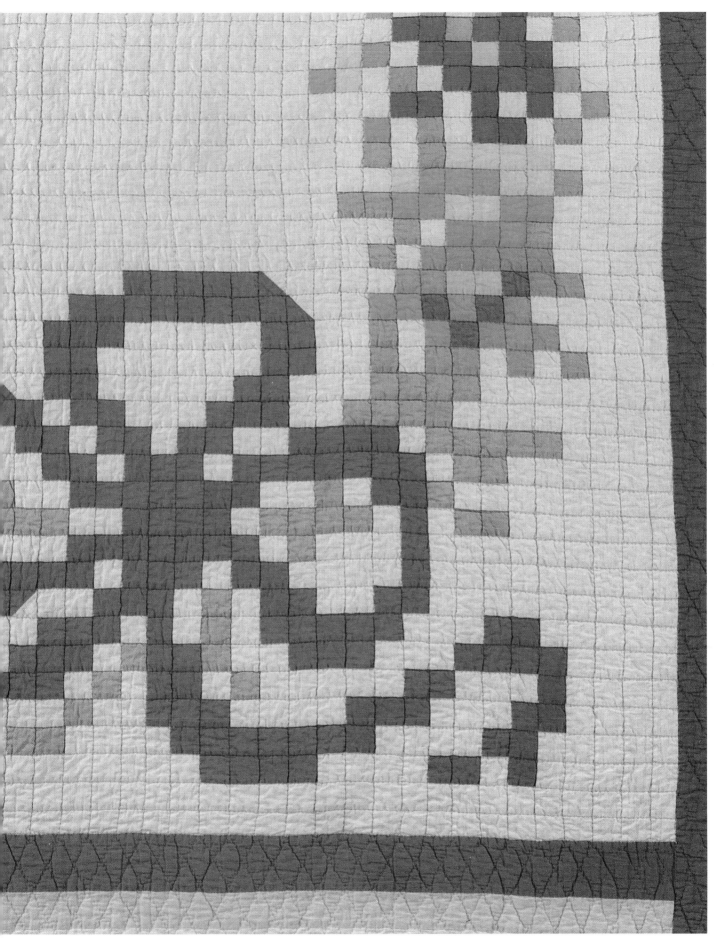

36. Detail of French Wreath (See illustration 45).

37. Plate 1 of Set J, *Cross Stitch Designs* by Anne Orr, mid-1920s.

38. Anne Champe Orr, 1930. Photo courtesy of J. Scott Grigsby.

In October 1914 she began a monthly column called "Collector's Department" in *Southern Woman's Magazine*. Each month she presented photographs and descriptions of antique or art objects such as glass, silver, jewelry, furniture, and dolls, many from her own collections. The April 1915 "Collector's Department" was devoted to old samplers, which she called "the first cross-stitching." The February 1915 column included a story, "The Quilt That Built a Battleship," written by Katherine Hopkins Chapman. In 1918 *Southern Woman's Magazine* ceased publication, but by then Anne Orr's needlework patterns were being sold worldwide. She then worked for J. P. Coats Thread Company and the Clark Thread Company designing crochet patterns.

It has often been written that Anne Orr's desire to design needlework patterns originated with a visit to a New York art store. She had examined a fine tablecloth priced at nine hundred dollars embroidered with mice and dogs. She thought those designs were totally inappropriate for a table cover.[2]

In the preface of one of her early cross-stitch pattern books, Anne Orr wrote, "The purpose is to give designs for their appropriate uses, and one will find them peculiarly adapted to the old colonial furnishings, now so much in vogue."

Everyone who knew Anne Orr said she did not do needlework herself; she was the designer. Although she valued artistic design, she wanted her designs to be simple enough for all needleworkers.

She wrote in the same preface:

A book on fancy work is often like a book of simple recipes—the designs look easy enough in the pictures, but the woman who seeks to develop the intricate patterns soon learns her mistake and puts the book down as impractical. The designs presented herein have been prepared especially with a view to simplicity of construction in order that even the novice may succeed.[3]

In 1917 she gathered about her a group of women in Nashville who carried out her various designs. Known as her "needlework cabinet," through the years they included dozens of women. Gedy Higgins interviewed one of these women while researching Anne Orr's life and accomplishments. Nancy Mattingly was a high school student when she made cross-stitch models for the Anne Orr Studio. She told Gedy Higgins that Anne Orr would oversee the work, and sometimes she made the needleworkers pull out threads because a certain color was not the desired shade.[4]

Anne Orr began writing for *Good Housekeeping* in November 1919. The editor wrote, "We are happy to announce that beginning with this number, Mrs. Orr, who stands preeminent in crochet work, will show her designs exclusively in *Good Housekeeping*. A series of articles has been planned for the coming year, covering various phases of this subject."[5] Anne Orr's needlework articles continued for twenty years until her retirement in 1940. Each article contained ordering information for the featured patterns, which eventually included all types of needlework. Through this national exposure, Anne Orr developed a lucrative mail order business.

Quilt patterns never exceeded traditional needlework patterns in Anne Orr's column in *Good Housekeeping*. In 1921 she offered her first "patchwork" pattern to *Good Housekeeping* readers: a bedspread and bureau scarf in a Mother Goose and Goslings design to be appliquéd and embroidered. At the time, *patchwork* was a term used for appliqué—one had to cut a design out of cloth, pin it on a muslin top, and cover the edges of the design with embroidery stitches.

Over the years Orr favored appliqué quilts over pieced quilts. Of the sixty-eight printed patterns for full Orr quilts in *Good Housekeeping* two are whole cloth, thirty are pieced, and thirty-six are primarily appliqué. Like other quilt designers of the 1920s and 30s, Anne Orr updated traditional quilt designs, but those are relatively few. Her pieced quilt patterns made of one-inch squares of color that look like cross-stitch designs are among her best known.

Often Anne Orr looked to natural forms for inspiration. For her appliqué quilts, flowers were the most frequent design sources: Lily of the Valley, Cosmos, Forget-Me-Not, Jonquil, Poppy, Iris, Dogwood, and Tulip. Often they were grouped together in garlands, wreaths, bouquets, sprays, or baskets and tied up with a bow knot.

39. Anne Orr quilt column in *Good Housekeeping,* January 1935.

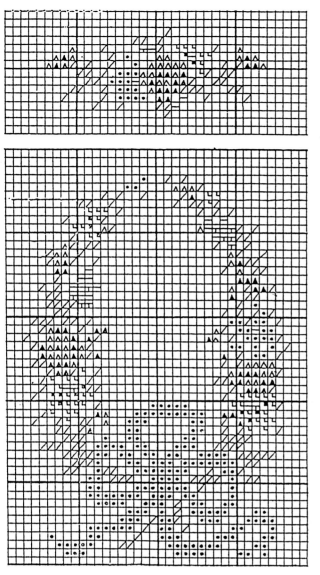

Color Chart

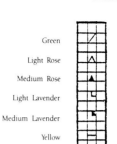

Green	
Light Rose	
Medium Rose	
Light Lavender	
Medium Lavender	
Yellow	
Tan	
Blue	

40. Working diagram and color insignia chart for French Wreath quilt from *Quilts and Quilting Set 100* by Anne Orr.

41. Anne Orr Studio logo.

The palette of colors she suggested for her quilts included soft pastels of eggshell blue, orchid, coral, mint green, and yellow. Her concern for color was so important that she devised ways that the needleworker would be sure to choose the correct gradation of color. Her color chart insignia for her cross-stitch-type quilt patterns were the same as ones in her cross-stitch patterns (See illustration 40). She often offered for sale fabric in the chosen color already stamped with cutting lines. In *Quilts and Quilting: Set 100,* her largest group of quilt patterns, she offered full-color photographs of the completed quilts so quiltmakers could match colors when buying fabric.

In addition to design and color choice, another striking characteristic of Anne Orr quilts is the central focus of her designs. She once wrote: "The most important piece of furniture in the bedroom is, of course, the bed. Therefore the most important accessory is the bedspread. Upon it the eyes are fixed on entering a bedroom, and upon it one's interest centers."[6] Marie Webster had also designed her quilts to fit the configuration of the bed.

In Orr's central medallion quilts, a large design fills the space below the pillows. Small strips of color often delineate the space surrounding the central design as in the Poppy pattern (See illustration 43). Often the section of the quilt that covers the pillows and the section that hangs down around the bed are treated as separate design units as in the French Wreath, Poppy, and Heirloom Basket.

Anne Orr's quilts came with exquisite quilting patterns. Quilting designs were stylized, modern, and intricate; and they were sold separately from the appliqué and piecing patterns. Again, the concern was for balanced designs appropriate to the quilt's eventual use. She encouraged intricate stitching and even suggested using a thin layer of wool for batting to make small quilting stitches easier.

Her traditional pieced quilt patterns seem out of place when one looks at her quilts as a whole. She may have offered them because her readers requested them or perhaps

42. Detail of Poppy.

43. POPPY

Makers: Nora, Winnie, and Euretha Irwin and Bonnie Carden. Andersonville, Anderson County, Tennessee, circa 1933.

Lender: Dr. Gordon Irwin, nephew of Winnie Irwin.

Appliqué: 82″ x 91½″; cotton: white sheeting with appliqué in solid pink, rose, and green; muslin back; pink bias binding; thin cotton batting; quilted in ½-inch diamonds in background areas, in scallops inside dividing strips, and by the piece in the appliqué motifs. Quilting thread is white except in leaf areas where thread is green.

This Anne Orr quilt pattern appeared in July 1932 *Good Housekeeping* along with a matching appliqué rug. To receive the hot-iron pattern with directions for appliqué, the reader sent fifty cents. With a central focus, a divided surface, and notched edge, this Anne Orr quilt pattern is artistically designed for the bed.

because her competitors were selling them. Anne Orr's Double Wedding Ring, Flower Garden, Aster, Drunkard's Path, and Star of Bethlehem (all popular 1930s quilt patterns) are just as carefully designed as her fancy appliqué designs. Only two patterns were made up in popular print fabrics; instead, she suggested the solid pastel fabrics for which Orr quilts were famous.

Because Anne Orr is so well-known for her cross-stitch embroidery patterns, her quilts that look like cross-stitch are most often associated with her. Whether or not Anne Orr originated the idea of transferring the "squared off" look of cross stitch to quilt designs is difficult to determine. Cuesta Benberry pointed out that the squared off look was not unusual in the first part of the twentieth century, as that kind of design, using graph paper, was taught in art classes in schools nationwide, even at the elementary level.[7]

However, it is safe to say that Anne Orr popularized the idea when her first squared off patterns were published in *Quilts and Quilting: Set 100*, in 1932. Two quilts in the set used the construction: French Wreath (See illustration 45) and the Dresden quilt. Women who bought the pattern pamphlet received a working diagram and a color insignia chart like one in a cross-stitch pattern. Each square on the working diagram represented a one-inch square of plain-colored cloth. The pattern directions suggested making up ten-square-inch units of one-inch-square blocks, then joining the units together. The color chart eliminated the need for making decisions on colors and shading, but the construction process was an extremely tedious one. The center of the French Wreath quilt and its pillow sections are made of 2,680 pieces.

44. Venice Margaret Bussey Stokstad, 1935.

45. FRENCH WREATH

Maker: Venice Margaret Bussey Stokstad. Owosso, Michigan, 1935–1936.

Lender: Beth Dyer, daughter.

Pieced: 70″ x 81″; cotton: pink, blue, white, and various other solid pastels; white cotton back; pink bias binding; cotton batting; diamond quilting in sashing, overlapping circles in plain blocks, and by the piece in the center medallion; white quilting thread.

Special thanks to Susan Ciebell, daughter of the maker, for providing her mother's quilt story.

Using an Anne Orr pattern, Venice Bussey worked two years piecing the quilt in the evenings spent with other teacher friends in Michigan. In the summers, she returned home to Edgerton, Wisconsin, where she quilted this quilt on her grandmother's old frame.

Venice Margaret Bussey Stokstad (b. 1902)

Venice Bussey's parents, Ezra and Mary, lived on Mary's family farm in Edgerton, Wisconsin. The family had hired immigrant girls from Scandinavia to help on the farm; and after the chores were done, the girls would sit for awhile doing all types of needlework. From them and from her mother and grandmother, Venice learned hardanger, crewel, and cross-stitch. She also learned to piece quilts, making single quilt blocks first. The women made tacked quilts for everyday use out of cotton sacks. Hers was a prosperous family, but very economical.

When the Depression hit, the family was no longer able to have hired help. Venice went to the University of Wisconsin where she met her future husband, Lewis Stokstad. He graduated with a degree in agriculture, and she had a degree in English. Neither could find a job near home, so they postponed their marriage. Lewis went on the fair circuit showing cattle, and Venice took a job teaching in Owosso, Michigan. In 1937 they were married in Wisconsin.

The Heirloom Basket quilt was one of four cross-stitch-type designs featured in the January 1935 issue of *Good Housekeeping* (See illustration 47). The others were Oval Wreath, Debutante's Pride, and Star Flower.[8] The color gradation was so important to the success of the designs that the Orr Studio offered a full-color photograph with the purchased pattern.

Other cross-stitch-type designs appeared in *Good Housekeeping*: the Marie Antoinette quilt,[9] the Early American Wreath,[10] the Cross Stitch quilt,[11] the Pieced Quilt with Blue Border,[12] the Bow Knot quilt, and the Quaint Pieced quilt.[13] Completed quilts made from these cross-stitch-type designs are rarely found, probably because of the length of time needed to make them; but they delight today's viewers who think the quilts look like patterns digitalized by computers.

Stearns and Foster included on their 1940 Mountain Mist batting wrapper some quilt patterns inspired by Anne Orr designs. Roses Are Red, number 66, and Cross Stitch Garden, number 42, are made of one-inch squares of fabric constructed in the cross-stitch process. Whether or not Anne Orr was paid for the patterns is not clear, but they are not attributed to her.

At least two quilts made from Anne Orr's quilt patterns received awards at the 1933 Chicago World's Fair Sears National Quilt Competition (See illustration 46). One was an adaptation of Autumn Leaf, an appliqué pattern Anne Orr featured in her January 1930 *Good Housekeeping* column.[14] A simplified version appeared in her *Good Housekeeping* article in January 1932.[15] With concentric sections emanating from the center, the quilt has the central focus that Anne Orr patterns are known for. In 1930 the Orr Studio offered a hot-iron transfer pattern and directions for cutting out and placing the leaves and vines that meander around the center and side sections of the Autumn Leaf quilt. A quilting pattern was offered separately. The cost for the two patterns was seventy-five cents. For the simplified version in January 1932, she offered a three-dollar kit that included plain and printed fabric stamped to cut, a placing design, and bias-fold tape for stems. The top and lining were not supplied. Although this quilt is characteristic in style and design of other Anne Orr appliqué designs, the use of print fabric for the leaves in Autumn Leaf is a departure.

While the Autumn Leaf quilt did not win one of the top prizes, it was included in *Sears Century of Progress in Quilt Making*, a book of winning quilt patterns. It was called Autumn Leaves,[16] and it became a popular quilt pattern through its exposure in this publication. One wonders if Orr, a judge at the competition, disqualified herself when one of her patterns was judged.

Another Anne Orr design, the Lincoln quilt, won the regional Sears quilt competition in Memphis and was exhibited at the Sears Building at the Chicago World's Fair in the summers of 1933 and 1934 (See illustration 63). Anne Orr published this pattern and six other designs in color in the January 1933 issue of *Good Housekeeping* just five months before the entry deadline. Inez Ward of Horse Cave,

46. Judges pose in front of winning quilts at Sears regional contest in Kansas City, 1933. Autumn Leaf quilt in center won first prize for Mary Hilliker of Carl Junction, Missouri, who used an Anne Orr quilt design. The quilt was displayed at the Chicago World's Fair, and an adaptation of the pattern was sold nationally by Sears, Roebuck and Company. Photo courtesy of Spencer Museum of Art.

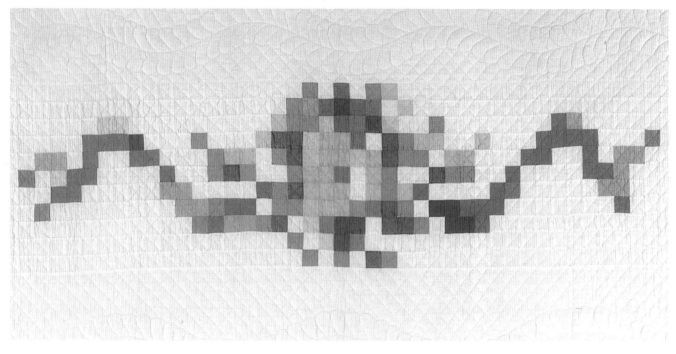

47. Detail of Heirloom Basket.

48. HEIRLOOM BASKET

Makers: Elizabeth Bates Greer (piecing) and Dolly Mae Long
(quilting).
Lancaster, Kentucky, 1935.

Lender: Dr. Don Graham.

Pieced: 69″ x 91½″; cotton: solid pastels and white; white percale
back; blue bias binding; quilted in ¾″ squares, parallel lines ¼″
apart and plumes; wool batting; quilting thread is white.

Elizabeth Bates Greer pieced the Heirloom Basket using an Anne
Orr pattern in the January 1935 issue of *Good Housekeeping.* Quilt
designs that look like cross-stitch are most often associated with
Anne Orr although other quilt designers made similar patterns.

Dolly Mae Long (1872–1955)

Dolly Mae Long and her husband married when she was sixteen
and he was eighteen. They raised five children, supporting them
with income from their farm in Kentucky and Dolly's quilting for
out-of-state customers. She is remembered by her niece as easy-
going, likable, and very refined. She was an immaculate
housekeeper and would always cover the quilt she was working on.
Elizabeth Greer obviously chose one of the best quilters in the
South when she asked Dolly Long to quilt the Heirloom Basket
quilt.

Elizabeth Bates Greer (circa 1880–circa 1960)

Elizabeth Bates was born in Woodbury, Tennessee. Her father died
when she was very young, but her mother was able to send
Elizabeth to the very fashionable Ward's Seminary for Girls in
Nashville. She also attended Vanderbilt University. Her mother died
before she graduated. At Vanderbilt her roommate contracted
tuberculosis, and Elizabeth had spots on her lungs.

The man she was to marry had a post in Cuba with the
Methodist Church. When he took her there for health reasons, she
recovered. They lived there several years and raised two daughters
born in 1903 and 1905. The couple later returned to Kentucky
where he was a presiding elder for the Methodist Church in the
Lancaster, Kentucky, area.

Her daughter, Frances Davies, remembers that Elizabeth loved to
do intricate needlework, especially embroidery and drawn work.
"She'd tackle almost anything. She did it because she enjoyed it."
She liked the pastel colors, especially blue. Elizabeth continued to
do needlework up to the last moment of her life.

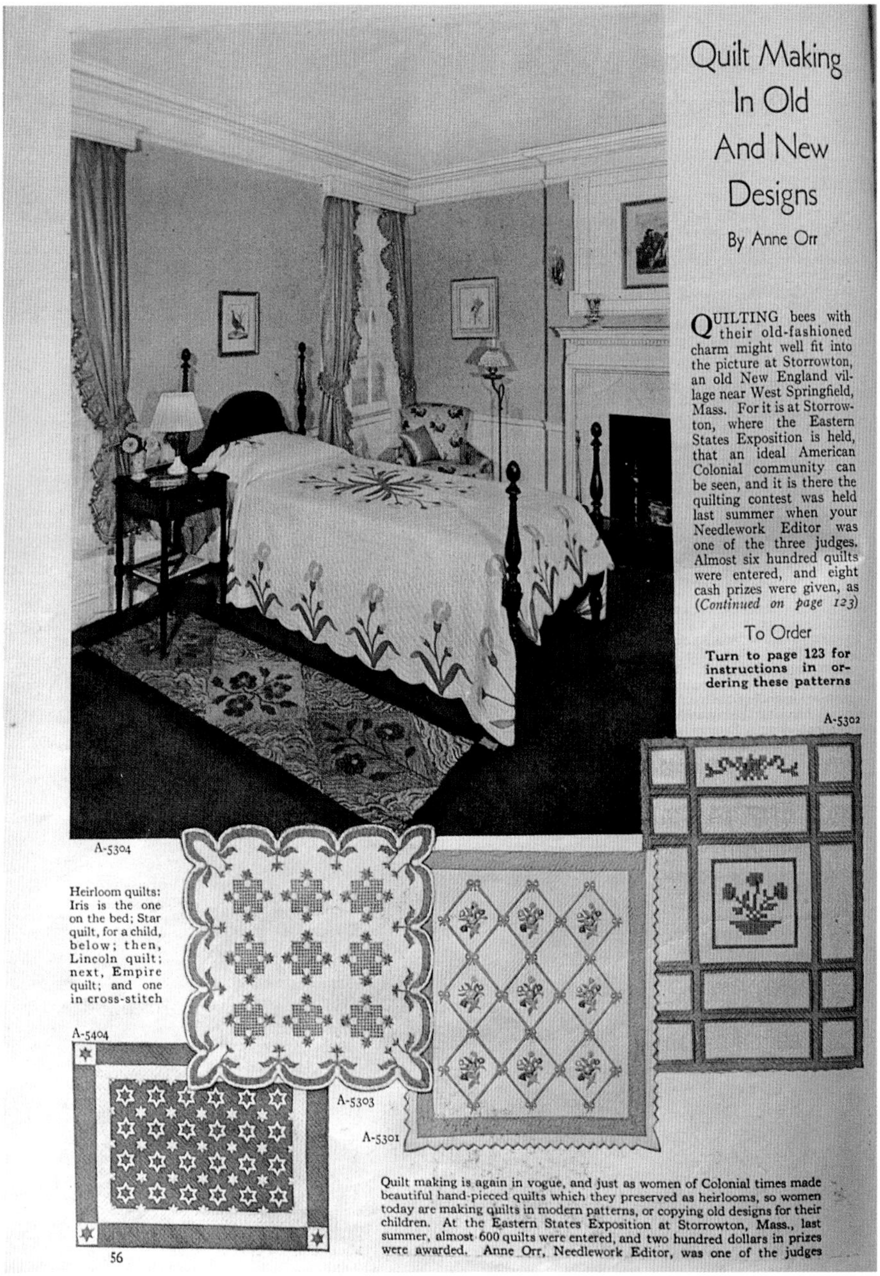

Quilt Making In Old And New Designs

By Anne Orr

QUILTING bees with their old-fashioned charm might well fit into the picture at Storrowton, an old New England village near West Springfield, Mass. For it is at Storrowton, where the Eastern States Exposition is held, that an ideal American Colonial community can be seen, and it is there the quilting contest was held last summer when your Needlework Editor was one of the three judges. Almost six hundred quilts were entered, and eight cash prizes were given, as (*Continued on page 123*)

To Order

Turn to page 123 for instructions in ordering these patterns

A-5302

A-5304

Heirloom quilts: Iris is the one on the bed; Star quilt, for a child, below; then, Lincoln quilt; next, Empire quilt; and one in cross-stitch

A-5404

A-5303

A-5301

Quilt making is again in vogue, and just as women of Colonial times made beautiful hand-pieced quilts which they preserved as heirlooms, so women today are making quilts in modern patterns, or copying old designs for their children. At the Eastern States Exposition at Storrowton, Mass., last summer, almost 600 quilts were entered, and two hundred dollars in prizes were awarded. Anne Orr, Needlework Editor, was one of the judges

56

49. Anne Orr quilt column in *Good Housekeeping,* January 1933.

Kentucky, made the quilt, but she did not remember where she got the pattern or who the designer was.

The Lincoln quilt takes its inspiration from quilts made in the mid-nineteenth century. In fact, Anne Orr wrote that the Lincoln Quilt was a copy of one owned by Lincoln's mother. Its tradition and story were printed in pamphlet number A-5303, which cost twenty-five cents. The appliquéd swag border is typical of fancy quilts of the mid-nineteenth century. The quilt does not have a central focus; instead, it consists of blocks featuring a center diamond made up of small squares.

The Lincoln quilt pattern was reprinted in 1942 in the *Lockport Quilt Pattern Book* published by the Lockport Cotton Batting Company of Lockport, New York, which also published a pattern called Cross Stitch Bouquet and another called the McGill Cherry quilt. Both are similar to other Orr quilt patterns.

Among embroidery enthusiasts, Anne Orr's name is still well known. Among quiltmakers and quilt collectors, she is not as well known. *Anne Orr Patchwork* (1977) by Jean Dubois, featured several of Orr's best-loved patterns with instructions; but it is now out of print. Of course, illustrations of her quilts in *Good Housekeeping* articles are available in some library collections, but for the most part her patterns are not usually identified as Anne Orr patterns. When state quilt project volunteers documented quilts, Anne Orr patterns were generally not identified because the most-used encyclopedias of quilt patterns do not include her patterns.

The quilts featured here are only five of about seventy known quilt designs she produced. The Nashville Public Library owns two albums of black and white photographs of Anne Orr quilts, probably once used by the Anne Orr Studio for publicity purposes. This remains the best source of Anne Orr quilt designs. The search for Anne Orr quilts is much easier with this set of Nashville photographs. For example, the Poppy and the May Basket quilts appeared unattributed in *A People and Their Quilts* by John Rice Irwin.[17] When I contacted one of the quiltmakers, she did not know the quilt was an Anne Orr design, saying "We just thought they were beautiful. My mother-in-law always subscribed to magazines, and she probably saw the pattern in *Good Housekeeping*."[18]

Anne Orr pattern instructions and transfers have surfaced as the search for Anne Orr quilts has progressed. Euretha Irwin still has her original tissue paper placement chart for her May Basket appliqué (See illustration 50). Ruth Snider of Independence, Kansas, saved patterns and shared them with others for years. Cuesta Benberry, a quilt historian for more than thirty-five years, remembers corresponding with Ruth Snider about an Anne Orr pattern: "Those were the days before Xerox machines. Ruth sent me the pattern through the mail. I copied the big tissue paper pattern onto another sheet of paper and sent the pattern back to her"[19] Fortunately, in the 1930s Anne Orr donated to the Tennessee State Library and Archives in Nashville a nearly complete set of her needlework and quilt designs printed through 1932.

Anne Orr comes across in her writing as a highly cultured, well-traveled woman with sophisticated taste in decorating. In Nashville she was considered a very successful businesswoman. As one learns more about Anne Orr's business success, one can easily become interested in her personality and the life she lived.

Born into a wealthy Nashville family in 1875, Anne Champe was educated at Price's School for Young Ladies and studied art under Sarah Ward Conley, a Nashville artist who had studied with French artist Julien Bouguereau. In 1894 she married John Hunter Orr, also from a wealthy native Tennessee family, who owned a highly successful wholesale grocery business with his four brothers. The Orrs had three daughters—Mary Hunter, Virginia Claiborne, and Anne Champe—who were already married when their father died in 1928. By that time Mrs. Orr's needlework studio had been in operation for more than ten years. She continued to write for women's magazines and to publish patterns until her death in 1946.

50. Euretha Irwin of Andersonville, Tennessee, holds her May Basket quilt made from an Anne Orr pattern, which included transfer patterns for the cutting templates and a tissue paper placement chart for the appliqué pieces. She began the quilt in 1936 and finished it in 1938.

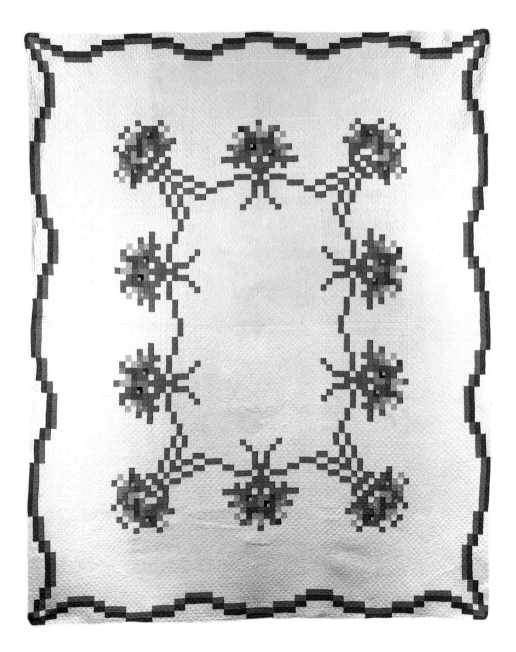

51. NOSEGAY

Maker: Unknown, early 1930s.

Lender: Dr. H. L. Durrett, grandson of Martha Villines Winfield who gave him the quilt in 1931.

Pieced: 78″ x 94″; cotton: solid pastels and white; blue percale back; white bias binding; cotton batting; quilted in ⅝″ diamonds in center panel quilting and running vine in border. Quilting thread is white.

This quilt pattern is similar to Anne Orr patterns; however, no printed pattern has been found. One significant difference from Orr's designs is that not all the squares are the same size. In this quilt, a yellow ½″ square accents the flower buds. Martha Villines Winfield (1847–1934) may have made the quilt when she lived in Chicago (1918–1928), but more likely it was a gift to her.

52. Anne Champe Orr in her Packard in front of her home at 130 Twenty-first Avenue South, in Vanderbilt University area of Nashville, 1930. Photo courtesy of Anne Callahan.

53. Anne Orr with granddaughter, Anne Catherine Callahan, 1923. Photo courtesy of Anne Callahan.

As a young girl, Andrena Phillips lived across the street from Anne Orr's big house at 130 Twenty-first Avenue South in the Vanderbilt University area of Nashville. Her memories further an understanding of Anne Orr.

I remember at age six [in 1922] taking a ride with Miss Anne in her electric car. It was the first electric car in Nashville. It looked like the queen's carriage in England. Miss Anne always looked queenly. She had beautiful white hair and always dressed in black. She wore a little black hat and a high lace neck band.

It was always fun to go into her house. She had a house man—we called him Brown. He was very courtly. He waited on the table, wore a white coat, answered the door, polished silver, and so forth. You might call him a butler, but he did much more than that. She also had a cook and a maid. She lived elegantly.

I don't think Anne Orr knew anything about a needle. My mother told me that. I thought that was strange that someone could do all those needlework patterns without knowing a bit about the needle.

She was something for her day because women didn't usually do this sort of thing. At finishing school she learned painting and china painting; I suppose it all branched out from that. To make a business out of it was unheard of.

She was a grande dame. She lived in a very affluent style. She collected beautiful silver and had portraits of had little curio tables all over the house with little glass cases covering art objects. She had a large number of miniatures she collected on her travels. The London Museum and Metropolitan Museum of Art in New York kept in touch with her about her miniature collection.

The shop was in the basement of her house. It was a nice little needlework shop run by her daughters Mary Hunter and Anne Champe. They sold needlework supplies and Anne Orr's designs. Her house was torn down after she died. Today a pancake restaurant stands where her great old house once stood.[20]

As a quilt designer Anne Orr was certainly not the most prolific, but her designs were some of the most innovative. As a designer, she was obviously aware of the strong national trend to Colonial Revival decorating, and she created designs that were both modern and traditional. As an entrepreneur, she successfully marketed her patterns for the sophisticated modern woman whose interest in quilts was not necessarily for warmth and comfort, but rather for beauty and style. Her impact on quiltmaking through her writing and judging of contests was certainly significant, but as a successful business woman at a time when it was not common for women to do such things, she was a pioneer.

SEARS NATIONAL QUILT CONTEST, 1933

Promoting the Tradition

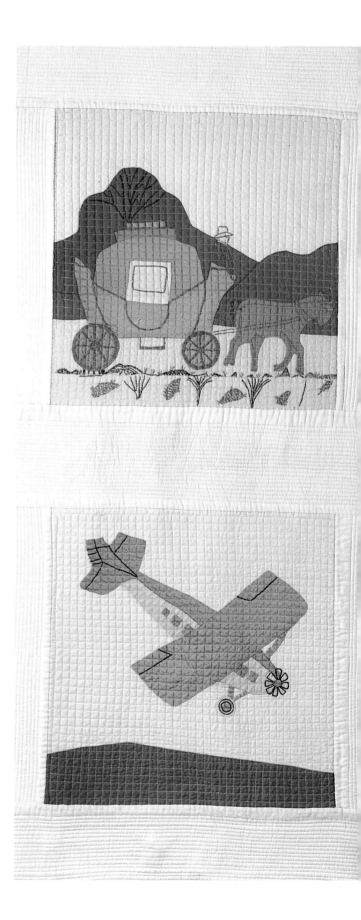

The Chicago World's Fair of 1933, known as the Century of Progress Exposition, was a greatly expanded version of a county fair: exhibits of foreign cultures, art exhibits, exhibits of the latest inventions, amusement rides. All were packaged to attract millions of visitors.

Sears, Roebuck and Company constructed a grand building just inside the fair entrance and invited the Sears family of customers and friends to make the Sears Building their home at the Fair, a place to meet, rest, eat, or write. Inside the building they promised exhibits of merchandise and manufacturing processes, but the customer would not be asked to buy anything![1]

One of the exhibits proved to be one of the company's most successful marketing ideas that year. Six months prior to the opening of the fair, it announced a national quilt competition with $7,500 in prizes, with the winning quilts displayed in the Sears Building at the fair. The exhibit would add to the homelike atmosphere Sears wanted to create, and it would certainly promote sales of fabric and quilt patterns.

Thirty winning quilts from the Sears local and regional contests held from May through June 1933 were exhibited in the Sears Building. Anne Orr was one of four judges. The quilt exhibit attracted so many visitors that Sears asked some of the quiltmakers to exhibit their quilts again in 1934.

54. Detail of Century of Progress (See illustration 61).

The contest was announced in newspaper advertisements, mail-out brochures, and the *Sears, Roebuck and Company Catalog* in early 1933. The rules for the contest were simple. Anyone could enter except employees of Sears, Roebuck and Company. Patchwork quilts of original or traditional designs that had never been exhibited were eligible. Antique quilts were discouraged. By the deadline of May 15—just five months later—more than 24,000 quilts had arrived at Sears stores.

Capitalizing on its nationwide system of retail and mail order outlets, Sears was able to provide a convenient entry system for the quilts. Quiltmakers took their quilts to their local Sears retail store or sent them to their Sears mail order house. Each retail store chose three top winners, and the ten mail order outlets chose ten winners to send to a regional contest.

For awarding prizes, Sears divided the country into ten regions centering at Chicago, Philadelphia, Boston, Kansas City, Minneapolis, Memphis, Atlanta, Dallas, Los Angeles, and Seattle. The three winners in each region were then sent to Chicago to compete for the national prize.

Winners at the local level were awarded first, second, and third prizes of ten, five, and five dollars respectively. Winners at the ten mail order houses were awarded five prizes of ten dollars each and ten prizes of five dollars each. Through the mail order outlets, five times as many prizes were awarded because Sears expected more quilts to be submitted by mail. The grand prize-winning quilt, made in eastern Kentucky, was submitted to the Chicago mail order outlet.

At the regional level, first, second, and third prizes of $200, $75, and $25 were offered. The three national prize winners were awarded $1,000, $500, and $300 respectively. The large amount of money certainly was an incentive few quiltmakers could resist.

55. Grand prize-winning quilt submitted by Margaret Rogers Caden on back cover of *Sears Century of Progress in Quilt Making,* 1934.

The grand prize-winning quilt was presented to Mrs. Eleanor Roosevelt at a ceremony that was duly photographed in the fall of 1933, but the quilt has disappeared since that time (See illustration 55).

The contest rules stipulated that a bonus of $200 would be given to the grand national prize-winner if the quilt design commemorated the theme of the Century of Progress. Many quilts with the Century of Progress theme were submitted, but none won a regional contest. These Century of Progress theme quilts were covered with original appliqué motifs pertaining to historical events, advances in transportation, and so forth. The winning quilts, on the other hand, were traditional pieced and appliqué quilt designs.

At least one entrant who had made a theme quilt protested in a letter to Sears:

> I understand that the Century of Progress quilts or those featuring the progress of the last century are not being considered or given recognition over colonial designs, except that some are tagged "Honorable Mention." One of the judges was overheard to state she could not give three minutes of her time to consider a Century of Progress design. We spent considerable time, thought, and energy, not to speak of money, in our efforts to produce something worthwhile along the lines called for by your company.[2]

57. Detail of Lily of the Valley.

56. LILY OF THE VALLEY

Maker: Rebekah Ward DeWitt.
  Nashville, Davidson County, Tennessee, 1933.

Lender: Rebecca DeWitt Wright, granddaughter.

Appliqué: 73″ x 91″; cotton: medium green and white solids, light
  green background; light green back; medium green bias binding;
  cotton batting; quilted center medallion, small bouquets of lily of
  valley quilted in scallops, quilted by the piece in appliqué, and
  straight parallel lines in background.

Rebekah Ward DeWitt won second place in the local Nashville
Sears Quilt Contest in 1933 with her Bride's Quilt. This quilt, the
probable prize winner, represents the highly decorative style
favored by judges who were often interior designers and artists.

Rebekah Ward DeWitt (1873–1961)

Rebekah Ward was born into a family whose effect on Tennessee
history has been significant. Her father, William E. Ward, a
Presbyterian minister, founded Ward's Seminary for Girls in
Nashville after the Civil War. The family lived in a very fine house
on the campus. When her father died at age forty-eight, Ward's
Seminary was sold and renamed Ward-Belmont. Today it is
Belmont College, a four-year college supported by the Baptist
Church.

  Rebekah was educated at Ward's Seminary where she received art
training from her sister Sarah Ward Conley, a prominent artist who
studied under French artist Julien Bougereau. One of Rebekah's
best friends was Anne Champe Orr.

58. Rebekah Ward DeWitt of
Nashville, Tennessee.

  In 1899 Rebekah Ward married John H. DeWitt, an attorney. In
1925 he was appointed judge of the Tennessee Court of Appeals. His
hobby was Tennessee history, and he served as president of the Tennessee Historical Society for many years until his death in 1937. Rebekah continued as secretary of the organization until her death.

  Her son John DeWitt, Jr., made a name for himself in broadcasting.
As a nineteen-year-old, he got a job with the brand new WSM radio,
and in 1932 he became the station's chief engineer. He is credited with
coining the term "Grand Ole Opry."

  The DeWitts' older son Ward named his daughter after Rebekah.
Rebekah gave the Lily of the Valley quilt to her granddaughter, in-
scribed: Rebecca Jane DeWitt, March 3, 1934.

To appease these disgruntled quilters, a few Century of Progress quilts were exhibited at the Chicago World's Fair.

In Tennessee, quiltmakers had easy access to the contest through the Sears retail stores in Memphis, Nashville, and Knoxville; in rural areas, entrants simply sent their quilts to the nearest mail order outlet.

On May 22 and 23, 1933, *The Tennessean,* a Nashville newspaper, and Sears, Roebuck and Company had a public exhibition following the judging of the quilts. In a large advertisement, Sears announced the winners, their addresses, and the names of the quilts. Rebecca DeWitt of Nashville won second prize with a quilt called the Bride's Quilt. It is probably the Lily of the Valley quilt given to her granddaughter in 1934 (See illustration 56). Sprigs of white lily of the valley tied up in bows are appliquéd on pale green cotton fabric. The style of quilt is one favored by quilt designer Anne Orr; in fact, Rebecca DeWitt was a very close friend of Anne Orr, who may have given her design advice.

In addition to the three Nashville winners, all fourteen honorable mention winners were listed in the newspaper announcement.[3] At least two of them were Century of Progress theme quilts; two were untitled; and six were traditional designs such as Martha Washington's Flower Garden, Rising Sun, Star of Bethlehem, and so forth. One was simply called Eight Thousand Pieces.

The three Nashville judges were Mr. A. Herbert Rodgers, a designer and interior decorator; Mrs. Marcellus B. Frost, a prominent club woman active in historical preservation; and Mrs. Claude Waller, a beautification advocate. The women were prominent Nashvillians; and Mr. Rodgers, a graduate of the Chicago Art Institute, was the decorator of many of Nashville's finest homes. Interestingly, the judges chose three distinct types of quilts as the top three winners: a traditional Turkey Tracks, a stylized appliqué Lily of the Valley, and one called Pyrotechnics, which certainly sounds modernistic but was published in the Ladies' Art Company catalog around 1900.

In Knoxville, on May 14, 1933, the judges for the local contest were announced in the *Knoxville News-Sentinel.* Lillian Keller of the University of Tennessee Extension Division was the judge since she often judged contests at local, regional, and state fairs. She was well known as the supervisor of home demonstration agents throughout the state. According to Claire Gilbert, a colleague of Miss Keller, Miss Keller did not make quilts, but it was not unusual for her to be asked to judge such a contest.[4] Mrs. Daniel Briscoe and Mrs. H. R. Duncan, the other judges, were prominent Knoxville women.

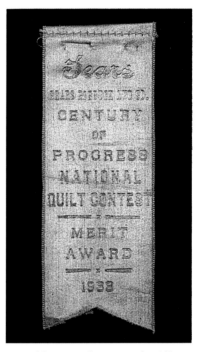

59. Ribbon won by Samantha Allison Wise in the Sears Century of Progress Quilt Contest.

60. Samantha Allison Wise with husband John of Knoxville, Tennessee, on the occasion of their fifty-fifth wedding anniversary, 1933.

61. CENTURY OF PROGRESS QUILT

Maker: Samantha Allison Wise.
  Knoxville, Knox County, Tennessee, 1933.

Lender: Susan Visconage Buerkens, great-granddaughter.

Pieced and appliqué: 71″ x 92″; cotton: cream, light blue, beige, and green solids; cream sateen back; blue-grey sateen straight binding; very thin batting; machine quilting in ½″ squares in appliqué blocks and ¼″ apart parallel lines in sashing using white thread.

This Century of Progress theme quilt won the Knoxville round of the Sears National Quilt Contest, but not the Atlanta regional contest where 1,100 quilts were judged. No theme quilts won regional prizes. Stylistically, judges seemed to be more impressed by the pretty, decorative quilts.

Samantha Allison Wise (1859–1937)

Samantha Allison married John R. Wise in Rural Vale in East Tennessee in 1878. In 1933 they celebrated fifty-five years of marriage that included raising nine children and founding a successful manufacturing company that produced rock crushers for flour mills.

Dorothy Watt remembers her grandparents' big, two-story frame house on Chilhowee Avenue in Knoxville. The Wises had hired help: two women named Pincie and Nina.

Samantha's granddaughter, Mary Rockette, remembers Samantha as a quiet, dignified person not given to idle gossip of any kind. She studied her Bible often and attended the Methodist church frequently, and she and her husband studied his Blue Book Speller to be sure they did not misspell a word or use it incorrectly. Mary Rockette remembers that her grandmother did beautiful hand work in sewing and made some exquisite quilts, but she does not know where they are.

One of the winning quilts in Knoxville was featured in a photograph in the May 28, 1933, issue of the *Knoxville News-Sentinel*. The third place quilt made by Mrs. J. R. Wise of Knoxville had a Century of Progress theme (See illustration 61). The Sears Building at the World's Fair is appliquéd at the center of the quilt. Surrounding the building are appliqué motifs showing the progress in transportation systems since 1833. Quilting was by machine, which might have reflected the fast approaching deadline. The Wise quilt carries with it a green ribbon embossed in gold with the words "Merit Award Sears Century of Progress National Quilt Contest 1933" (See illustration 59).

The *Knoxville News-Sentinel* did not announce the first and second place quilts, but at the Atlanta regional competition one of the Knoxville entries won a top prize and the honor of being displayed at the Sears Building at the fair. Mrs. Joe Wade of Knoxville won second prize for an appliqué "yellow iris with delicate shades of green."[5] Unfortunately, neither this quilt nor the quiltmaker's descendants have been located.

Eleven hundred quilts were sent to the Atlanta regional contest held on May 25, 1933. Three prominent Atlantans served as judges: Mr. Lewis Skidmore, director of the High Museum of Art; Mrs. Max Land, president of the Woman's Club; and Mrs. Julian Harris, artist and writer. They gave the first prize to the Star of France design. According to a reporter of the *Atlanta Constitution*, "The entire quilt formed a brilliant star in the various shades of yellow fashioned on a heavenly blue background. The exquisitely fine feather stitching proved to be the deciding factor for the judges." The third award went to an "antebellum-type" quilt in blue and white.[6]

The Sears, Roebuck and Company store in Atlanta was swamped with the 1,100 quilts entered in the regional contest. At first only 650 were exhibited, but two days later the other quilts were shown when the original 650 were taken down for packing.[7] Surely, seeing such a large number of quilts prompted many women to stop by the fabric department for materials for their next quilt projects.

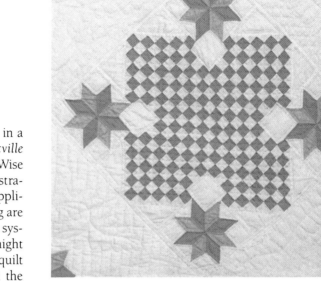

62. Detail of Lincoln Quilt.

63. LINCOLN QUILT

Maker: Inez Ward.
   Horse Cave, Kentucky, 1933.

Lender: Inez Ward.

Pieced and appliqué: cotton: white and pink; cotton batting; decorative quilting throughout.

Using an Anne Orr pattern borrowed from a friend, Inez Ward made this quilt and entered it in the Sears, Roebuck and Company National Quilt Contest. The quilt won first place at the Memphis Regional Contest and was exhibited at the Sears Building at the Chicago World's Fair in 1933. In the summer of 1934 the quilt was again exhibited at the Fair when organizers decided to extend the successful Fair for another year.

Inez Ward (b. 1911)

Inez Ward has lived her entire life in Horse Cave, Kentucky. At age seventeen, she married Louis Ward. Her husband worked for the state of Kentucky, but Inez's father wanted him to work on the family farm. Although her husband had not done farm work before, he agreed. When Inez received the news that she had won the first place Memphis regional prize of two hundred dollars in the Sears National Quilt Contest, her husband and father were plowing out in the cornfield. "I remember I ran out to them and told them. They were so excited. They brought the team to the house and decided that was enough work for the day." Inez had drawn off the pattern for her prize winning quilt from a friend's pattern. She cut the templates out of heavy paper. It was her first "fancy" quilt.

64. Cover of *Sears Century of Progress in Quilt Making.*

The Sears contest raised some questions that continue to cause concern today. The judges were looking for perfection in workmanship, beauty and harmony of color arrangement, and beauty of design; but knowing how to make a quilt was not a prerequisite for being a judge. Most of the judges were decorators, artists, and designers. Therefore, the question is: Who is the best judge of quilts—a designer, an artist, or a quiltmaker?

The contest raised other questions. What is an original quilt pattern? Should quilts made from kits be allowed? Should quilts made by more than one person be allowed? For instance, the grand prize-winning quilt was made by several women working for Margaret Rogers Caden of Lexington, Kentucky. Although Miss Caden paid the women their regular pay, they did not receive a share of the grand prize of one thousand dollars.[8]

At the Memphis regional contest, Inez Ward of Horse Cave, Kentucky, won the prize of two hundred dollars for her pink and white Lincoln quilt, an Anne Orr design (See illustration 63). The quilt traveled to the Chicago World's Fair where it was enjoyed by thousands of visitors, and the next summer it was again displayed when Sears decided to repeat its successful exhibit. One woman from California, having seen the quilt in Chicago, contacted Inez Ward and asked her to make a duplicate.

Studying the 1933 Sears contest at the local and regional levels provides quilt researchers a rich source of information about quiltmaking. Since the results were so extensively reported over such a short period of time (May 15 to June 15, 1933), it is relatively easy to locate newspaper accounts. Often articles contain names of quilts, quiltmakers' married names, judges' names, and occasionally even photographs of quilts.

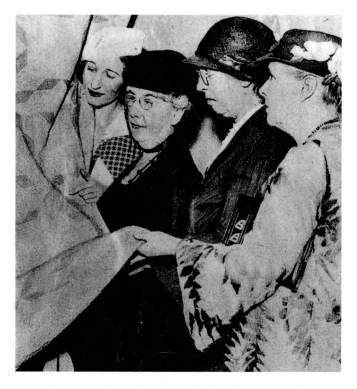

65. Judges Sue Roberts of Sears, Roebuck and Company, Anne Orr, Mary McElwain, and Beth Burnett of the Chicago Art Institute examine the grand prize-winning quilt at the 1933 Chicago World's Fair Sears Quilt Contest. Photo courtesy of the Spencer Museum of Art.

Despite all the behind-the-scenes intrigue, the contest prompted a furious amount of quiltmaking over the next decade. The Nashville Sears, Roebuck and Company staff summed up their enthusiasm in a newspaper announcement:

The Quilt-Making Contest has shown a wonderful revival in the most beautiful of Early American Arts. Quilt designs, once thought lost have been uncovered. New designs have been created. New color blending, new appliqué technique, new needlecraft . . . all have been introduced . . . to add to the progress made in Quilt-Making. In the contest, quilt designs of the most famous patterns, were used. The sentiment of generations ago is shown in a number of designs, copied from quilts, hundreds of years old. The improvements in the textiles, the publication of designs, and the educational arts, has given the woman of today a greater advantage over her ancestors. That advantage has been shown in the quilts submitted in this contest and the fact that in most every home, a quilt is in the process of making.[9]

Long after the contest had ended, Sears, Roebuck and Company continued to capitalize on the national contest by selling patterns of the winning quilts and pillows to match in a book of patterns called *Sears Century of Progress in Quilt Making* (See illustration 64).

A national quilt contest sponsored by *Good Housekeeping* was repeated for the 1939 New York World's Fair, but it did not enjoy the same success as Sears had. Quilts with the theme of "Better Living in the World of Tomorrow" were judged and displayed at Macy's department store in New York City. Traditional and antique quilts were excluded.[10] Compared to the 24,000 quilts entered in the Sears contest, the number of entries (600) in the *Good Housekeeping* contest seems minuscule. Again, Anne Orr was one of the judges.

Hard Times Quiltmaking

Interviews

Ironically, it took the hard times of the Great Depression to re-create "colonial times" for city dwellers who had become accustomed to the luxuries of the fast-paced modern times of the 1920s. In rural Tennessee, where the prosperity of the 1920s had not had a significant effect, families found it hard to see much difference between times before and after the stock market crash of 1929. Vacie Thomas's comment is not unusual: "We didn't know there was a depression—I'm not kidding. We were living like we always had."

Rural Tennessee women grew gardens, canned vegetables, raised chickens and hogs, and made quilts by the dozens. These women did not see themselves as noble pioneer women maintaining the old-fashioned craft of quiltmaking. They were simply doing what had to be done to fill a basic need.

Mail order catalogs, newspapers, and magazines, however, brought new products to the front rooms of Tennessee farm houses. Color-fast fabrics, designer patterns, time-saving gadgets, and thousands of mail order offers surely tempted the long-time quiltmaker.

To gauge the effect of commercialization on the traditional quiltmaking process, I chose to interview several women who had learned to quilt from a mother or grandmother and had made quilts during the 1930s. Asking people about their lives fifty-five years earlier can be risky since memories can fade or be embellished. Georgia Mize once commented on her slow response to a question on quiltmaking: "I'm sorry. My mind hasn't dwelled on that for a long time." Inez Ward replied to one of my questions, "It is hard to remember. A lot of things have happened to me since then. That can do something to you." Nevertheless, oral interviews can be a valuable supplement to historical accounts.

66. Detail of Wedding Ring (See illustration 80).

The interviews focused on the following topics: how the women learned to quilt, what materials they used, what processes they followed, what patterns they used, and what their standards for fancy quilts were.

Vacie Thomas remembers very much wanting to quilt when she was young, but her mother would not let her. "For meanness, or I don't know what, I got up under the quilt and bumped it. My mother thumped me on the head with her thimble. I haven't been up under a quilt frame since."

Ruth Reed of Greeneville, Tennessee, made a Nine Diamond as her first quilt. "My mother cut out the pieces, but I put them together. The first quilt I quilted on was a huge star."

Since string-quilt blocks sewn on a paper backing were easy to make, for many young girls a string quilt was their first attempt at quiltmaking (See illustrations 68, 69). Georgia Thomas Mize grew up on a Sevier County farm near the Smoky Mountains.

> My first memory of quilts was when I was real small. My mother was always sewing and quilting. I saw her doing it. I couldn't hardly hold a needle, I was so small. I kept on and on. My mother began to give me something to try. First I had to piece, and then I'd have to tear it out. I started out on paper—probably no pattern at all. I made quilts for the cats.

68. A 1930s quilt top made in the string quilt method on newspaper. Quilt top owned by Eva Earle Kent of Knoxville, Tennessee. Photography by Gary Heatherly.

67. Vacie Murphy Thomas of Chattanooga, Tennessee, quilting in 1986.

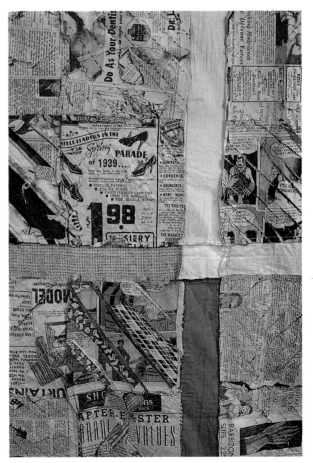

69. Back of string quilt top showing the newspaper backing that is removed before quilting begins. Photograph by Gary Heatherly.

[50]

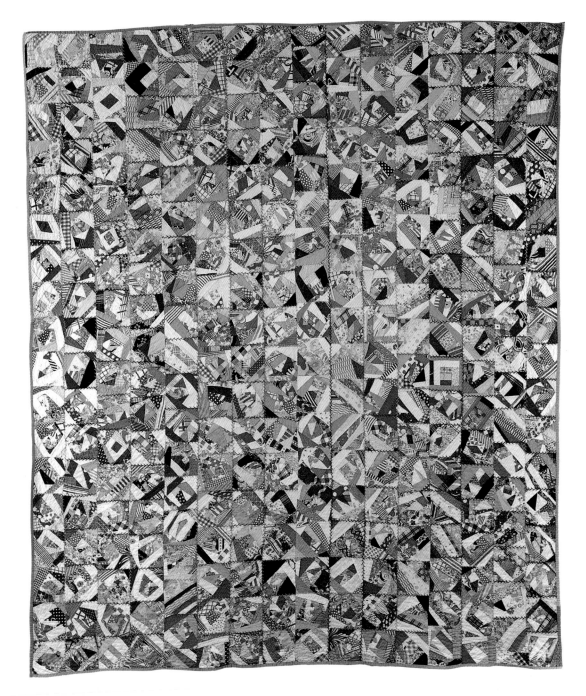

70. Detail of String Quilt.

71. STRING

Maker: Elva Wilson.
   Clifty Community, Cumberland County, Tennessee, 1930s.

Lender: Edna Gossage.

Pieced in the string method: 64″ x 75½″; cotton: assorted calico scraps; turquoise cotton back; turquoise straight binding; no batting; fan quilting; briar stitch embroidery accents the string piecing.

This is a spectacular example of string piecing. A "string" is defined as a piece of fabric that is too small to make anything from. Women sewed the strings down to a paper or cloth foundation before joining the string-pieced blocks together. The paper was taken off the back before the quilting began.

Vacie Thomas's mother made string quilt blocks on newspaper. "My mother would always want us to make them diagonal, but we didn't always do that."

Georgia Swanner was still making string quilts with feedsack cloth in the early 1940s before she got married (See illustration 72). "I had eight quilts and tops made to go when I married. In the country you could sleep under four or five quilts in one of those old houses."

I asked the women where their patterns came from. Talking about her mother's era, Georgia Mize said, "They didn't know there was such a thing, I don't guess, as a pattern back then. Every quilt that's been real old has been a pretty quilt with fancy quilting. I don't know how they did it."

When I asked her about patterns coming to her house, Georgia Mize replied, "There weren't any newspapers and magazines in our house. Wasn't able to buy them. [My mother] got a lot of ideas for her quilts from her mother—they were all great quilters. That's where she got her patterns. You can see I got my idea for my star quilt from one handed down from the 1800s."

Although Ruth Reed's family received the *Greeneville Sun* and several national magazines, they usually didn't order the quilt patterns. If someone did order one, she "would pass around patterns. We'd make the pieces out of sandpaper or out of stiff paper and pin them to the cloth. My brothers were carpenters and my granddaddy was a furniture maker, so we used sandpaper."

Georgia Swanner echoed Ruth Reed. She said, "A pattern'd get started out in the country, and they'd share them—one family to the next. One would cut it off on paper [newspaper, brown paper bag]. My mother, Ada Sutherland, and her neighbor Maybell Hendon—they'd share patterns more than anybody else around there. Maybell and Ada lived one and one-half to two miles apart."

Georgia Swanner continued: "Some would send away for a pattern out of the paper and magazines. It would cost ten cents or whatever—wasn't much back then."

Vacie Thomas's mother made dresses for her four daughters. "She would look in the catalogs for dress patterns, but she wouldn't order them. She had a standard pattern, so she would just make the alterations in the pattern by looking at the pictures of the latest dress styles in the catalogs." This dressmaking practice is similar to a quiltmaker adapting a pattern to her own preferences.

I asked Georgia Swanner if she had any favorite appliqué quilts. "I have an appliqué rose and a tulip pattern that I love to do. I just kindly used the pattern and made it to suit myself."

Georgie Mize got only one pattern from another state:

It was called Old-Fashioned Sweetheart. My older sister got a pattern of it, and then I made a pattern of it. I liked it quite well. I made it, I think, when I was thirteen years old. I had rheumatic fever. I couldn't do anything but sit, so I quilted. I put little birds and flowers on it. Kind of decorated it a little bit. I just did that to make it look pretty. I thought it looked pretty. My mind a doin' it I reckon. It was what I wanted to do.

72. Detail of String Quilt.

In 1935 Ruth Reed of Greeneville made her Broken Star quilt (See illustration 74). Broken Star quilt patterns were being sold throughout the country in kits of precut fabric diamonds, but Ruth Reed thought she could do that on her own.

I had received the pattern in color in the mail. You could write to the company for the pre-cut pieces of fabric, but I thought that was too expensive. So I cut up the paint chart strips in the *Sears, Roebuck Catalog* and chose my color combination. I cut out the color strips to see which went best together. Then I took my chosen colored strips to the J. C. Penney's store in Greeneville and bought broadcloth to match for ten cents a yard. Of course, it took a while figuring how much cloth to buy, but I thought it was worth it.

It took a year to piece it—probably two winters of working two to three months each year. It wasn't a hard quilt for me to make. Mother and I spent a month quilting it one winter. I won a third prize on the Broken Star at the Greene County Fair. It was a special quilt for me. It was nice to see my quilt at the fair. I always liked seeing the handwork on display.

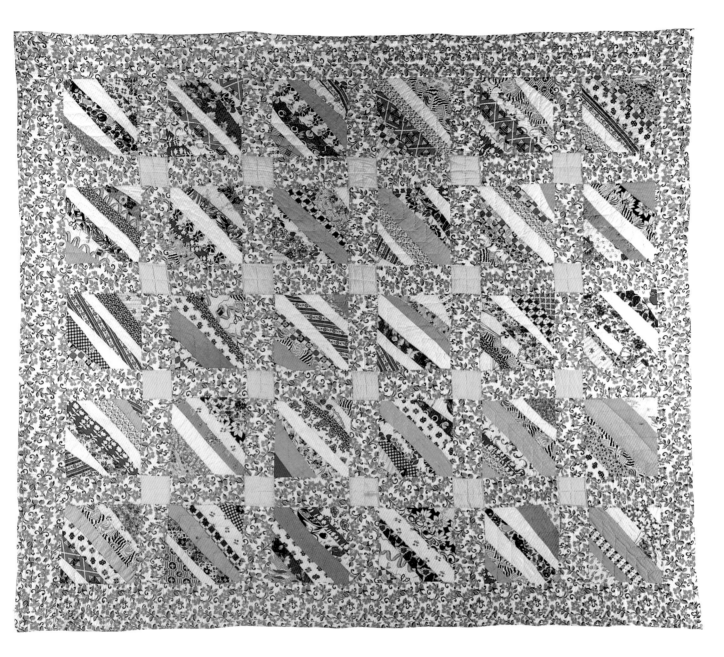

73. STRING

Maker: Georgia Sutherland Swanner.
   Sequatchie County, Tennessee, early 1940s.

Lender: Dot Davis.

Pieced in the string method: 72" x 86"; cotton: various figured feed
   and flour sacks; white feedsack back; edge is back turned to
   front; cotton batting; quilting is right angle quilting in blocks.

The quiltmaker grew up on a farm with nine siblings. She had one
school dress, which her mother made out of white flour sacks
which she "colored" with walnut hulls and red oak bark. The dress
was washed at the spring everyday after school. When she was a
young girl, Georgia learned to make tacked quilts out of overalls.
Later she learned to make string quilts on newspaper. This quilt
was one of several she had ready when she was married in 1946.

74. BROKEN STAR

Makers: Ruth Reed and her mother Lula Bible Reed.
  Greeneville, Greene County, Tennessee, 1935.

Lender: Sherry Edwards, niece of Ruth Reed.

Pieced: 64″ x 80″; cotton: broadcloth in rainbow colors and muslin;
  muslin back; cotton batting; red straight binding; cotton batting;
  quilted by the piece and in ¾″ squares in background using
  white thread.

In the mail Miss Reed received an order form for the Broken Star
pattern that included pre-cut pieces of cloth in the proper colors,
but Miss Reed thought it was too expensive. To find the right
combination of colors, she used the paint strip in the Sears,
Roebuck catalog and then went to the local J. C. Penney store to
purchase the broadcloth for ten cents per yard. Of course, she had
to figure the amount of cloth to buy; but she thought it was worth
it. Her quilt won third prize at a Greene County Fair in the 1930s.

Georgia Mize considers her World's Wonder quilt (See
illustration 76) one of her fancy quilts.

I call it World's Wonder—some people call it Postage
Stamp. My sister called it World's Wonder. She was making one so I made one. I don't know why, but whenever
you got a hold of a tiny piece of scrap you'd always make
some kind of quilt out of it. The smaller the piece the
fancier we thought it was. So that one is real fancy because the pieces are so small. On the back, I put a fancy
yellow lining—I thought it was back then. I ordered that
from Montgomery Ward. It was something special. Took
a long time to piece that. I don't remember how long. It
took more than a year.

In a family that needed dozens of quilts, purchasing quilt
fabric was expensive. Many women like Georgia Swanner's
mother made quilts from whatever textile they had.

During the Depression I was a young girl. We would put
together quilts from all kinds of fabrics. We made quilts
from pieces of overalls. We'd all sew together. We'd use

75. Georgia Thomas Mize of Sevierville, Tennessee, in 1986.

76. WORLD'S WONDER

Maker: Georgia Thomas Mize.
  Sevierville, Sevier County, Tennessee, 1930.

Lender: Georgia Thomas Mize.

Pieced: 63″ x 80″; cotton: assorted calico prints; yellow percale back; red straight binding; homegrown and hand-carded cotton batting; one-inch diamond quilting all over with white boss ball and white sewing thread.

Georgia Mize calls this her fanciest quilt. In the old days, she said, "The smaller the piece, the fancier it was." Compare this quilt to an Anne Orr pattern also made of hundreds of squares of cloth.

77. Full view of Four Patch and String.

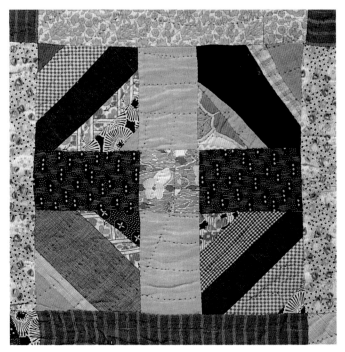

78. Detail of Four Patch and String.

79. FOUR PATCH AND STRING

Maker: Annie Belle Hodges Brown.
Sumner County, Tennessee, 1930s.

Lender: Tracy Brown, grandson.

Pieced: 65″ x 82″; cotton: denim and assorted scraps; home dyed
cotton back; filler is a burlap sack; edge is front to back on two
sides and back to front on two sides; allover fan quilting in black
thread.

Made of pieces of overalls, sewing scraps, and ticking, this quilt
represents the rough, utilitarian quilts made quickly to warm cold
bodies on a winter night in Tennessee. Thousands of these quilts
were made and worn out. Some people report sleeping under as
many as seven quilts, making it very difficult to roll over at night.
As meager as this quilt is, it is a proud record of quilting traditions
common to Tennessee families in the 1930s.

burlap bags for the filling. The burlap bags (called "tow
sacks,") were washed and sunned outside. We'd tack
these quilts. I learned to tack quilts at the age of seven or
eight. I learned to make string quilts pieced on newspaper when I was eleven or twelve years old. We'd use
odds 'n ends—scraps from making clothes, fertilizer
sacks, sugar sacks, feed sacks—anything.

Georgia Mize's sister was working on a WPA sewing project at the Red Cross Building in Knoxville. They were making overalls and dresses. "She'd bring us scraps. I guess we'd
have made lots of quilts, but we didn't have the scraps. We
got some awful pretty scraps from down there. Keep ourselves busy." The Wedding Ring quilt is made of those WPA
dress scraps (See illustration 80).

Many women like Mary Ellen Barding planted some rows
of cotton each year in her garden just for her quilts. Her
daughter, Mattie Jane Haun, said that if her mother was
short of cotton, she would use wool from sheep they raised
on the farm in Hamblen County.

Vacie Thomas and her sisters gathered leftover cotton
from the field after their father went to the gin. "We picked
out the seeds by hand and made batts for my mother's
quilts."

Georgia Mize remembers that in the winter "we would sit
in front of the fire and get the cotton warm. The seeds came
out easier that way. My mother would card it. She'd make
those little batts. We'd put that lining up to the quilt frame.

We'd lay those batts on it, and put the top on it and then
we'd be ready to go to work."

"My mother did a lot of fan quilting," continued Georgia
Mize. "She'd take a string with a piece of chalk and draw an
arc on the quilt top. I use a pencil on mine. Once she quilted
where you take a tea cup and put it like this and like that—
overlapping. Oh, she could quilt good! She was like me.
She'd like to sit with that needle."

Polly Dixon's mother always made her take nine stitches
on a needle. "I'd tell her I couldn't. She'd say, 'Try—try to
get as many as you can.' It made me keep my stitches small."

I asked the women what quiltmaking meant to them.
Ruth Reed responded quickly. "Quilting was something that
had to be done. I liked it because we didn't waste time. It
had a purpose. It had some benefit. I felt close to my mother
because we quilted for so many years together. I'd hear so
much about the olden times because I was with her all the
time."

Polly Dixon replied to the question: "I love to piece quilts.
It's a joy. It's an art within. It's very intriguing to put those
pieces together and see them come together."

Georgia Mize summed up the reactions of several others:
"I just liked it. I don't know why."

For many women, quilting is remembered fondly as a social activity. Georgia Swanner said, "Back then the women
used to have quiltings. They'd go to one person's house and
quilt 'em out. That's how they got things made back then. It

was like a club. They'd take casseroles. They'd share scraps and blocks amongst one another. That's how they came out with lots of colors."

Margaret Blackman Davis still lives near the small East Tennessee town of Philadelphia. She described her weekly "quilting." One woman in the remote rural area had a car. She would pick up her quilting friends and their preschool children, and they would all go to one woman's house to quilt. "It was great fun. When a quilt was almost finished, someone would say 'looks like we're gonna have to shake the cat.' And, yes, we did that—we used to bounce a cat on a finished quilt just off the frame!" It was a superstition that the person whose shoulder the cat leaped over would be the next to marry.

81. Georgia Mize and her brother Jimmie often played country music on a popular radio program in the 1940s.

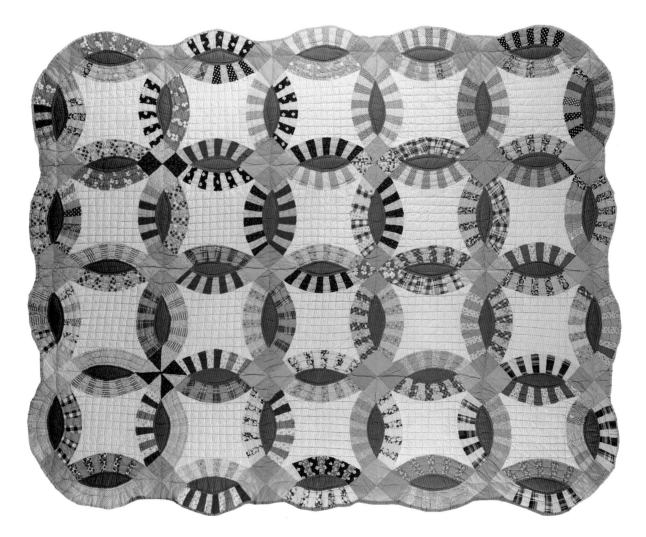

80. WEDDING RING

Maker: Georgia Thomas Mize.
 Sevierville, Sevier County, Tennessee, 1934.

Lender: Georgia Thomas Mize.

Pieced: 65″ x 81″; cotton: assorted calico prints and brown domestic; white flour sack back; pink straight binding; cotton batting; quilting in parallel archs in pieced rings and one-inch diamond quilting in plain centers; white cotton quilting thread.

The printed cotton fabric in this quilt came from a WPA sewing project in Knoxville. The Wedding Ring pattern is based on a nineteenth-century pattern called Pickle Dish. In its twentieth-century version, Wedding Ring became one of the most popular quilt patterns.

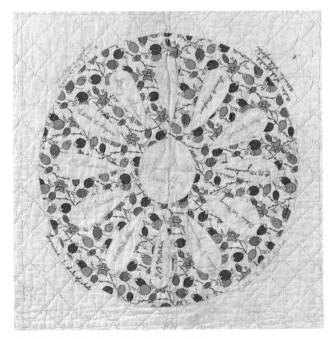

82. Detail of St. James Fundraising Quilt.

83. ST. JAMES EPISCOPAL CHURCH QUILT

Makers: Women's Guild of St. James Episcopal Church. Knoxville, Knox County, Tennessee, 1929.

Lender: Frances Dunlap, daughter of the church's rector.

Pieced and appliqué: 70″ x 84″; cotton: white and blue solids and a geometric print; white cotton back; blue straight binding; cotton batting; diamond quilting in background and border and quilted by the piece in the medallions; reverse appliqué in the medallions; names and date embroidered in various colors of thread.

In 1929 to raise funds for the mortgage payments on the two-year-old church building, the Women's Guild of St. James Episcopal Church sold doughnuts and bricks and made this quilt. Each woman was given a block to fill up with names of donors who gave fifty cents and wrote their names in pencil on labels. The women then transferred the names to the cloth and embroidered the names. They all got together to quilt the top. It was considered a very successful moneymaking venture. The finished quilt was given to the Rev. and Mrs. Eugene M. Hopper as a gift. Names of many well-known Knoxvillians, including the mayor of Knoxville at the time, are on the quilt.

Sarah Raley remembered her fellow textile mill workers making friendship quilts for one other. "They would each make a block and put their names on the blocks. They would be given to one worker—she would make a quilt out of them. This was not just done when a worker moved, had a baby, and so forth. It was just for friendship."

When I asked about the hard times, Lois Hall told me what women did to come up with cash. "People had chickens, but no money. The general store would take eggs in trade. For two eggs you could get a tablet and pencil. When the Baptist Church burned, they collected chickens to rebuild the building. Women raised five or six turkeys for their child's coat and shoes. I picked blackberries—had to walk two miles. I sold them for ten cents a gallon to a fella who made wine. We'd also raise a little cotton. We'd raise it to buy shoes. The tobacco we raised we got only one cent per pound, and we'd have to take it to Knoxville."

Sarah Raley lived up in the mining area north of Knoxville. "When hard times hit, it wasn't so bad because everybody was in the same boat. You had to cut corners. Everybody else was having trouble too. I'd go twice to the store for fifteen cents a woman gave me. I'd carry her kerosene lamp to be filled and a grocery basket over the other arm. I'd save those fifteen cents, and I'd buy a roll of remnants or I'd save them for something else I would want."

Sarah Raley continued, "From a kid up, I did it. I was used to it. I didn't spend it. In our town if you had a screen door, you were up in society. I'm proud of myself that I had the experiences I had. It was either 'root hog or die'—look out for yourself. I had to do it. There was no other choice."

Ruth Reed responded to the question about hard times: "I feel fortunate to have lived in hard times. It makes me appreciate the conveniences we have today."

The answers from the rural quiltmakers were remarkably similar. Quilts were made quickly with materials on hand. Sacks and worn-out clothing were the most common sources of fabric. Patterns were rarely purchased but were copied and passed around among quiltmakers. Homegrown cotton was used as the quilt filling. Quilting designs were as simple as fan quilting and parallel lines, and quiltmaking was a pleasure. In many ways they were living the "colonial life" romanticized by the advertisers. They were simply following a tradition passed down from pre-industrial days by their mothers and grandmothers.

With the beginning of World War II came the end of the Great Depression, and employment opportunities for these women improved dramatically. Georgia Mize moved to Knoxville where she sewed tents for the United States Army. Sarah Raley moved to Detroit to work in the defense industry. After work, she gathered tin cans and rubber tires to help in the war effort. Georgia Swanner got a job at a hosiery mill and later went to barber school. She retired in 1979 after thirteen years of cutting men's and women's hair. Vacie Thomas moved with her husband to Oak Ridge, Tennessee, where the atomic bomb was being developed. Lois Hall first got a job in the hosiery mill near her farm, but later she worked at Oak Ridge where she shared a dormitory room with women from other parts of the country.

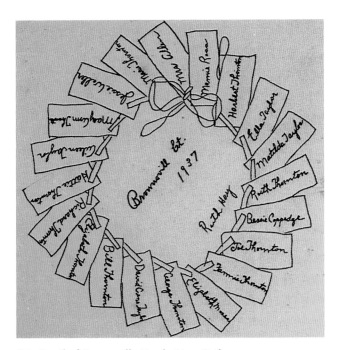

84. Detail of Brownsville Fundraising Quilt.

Mary Claiborne Mann (1873–1937)

Mary Mann was head of the missionary society for the Brownsville circuit of Methodist churches. She often made quilts, sold them, and gave the money to the district office, which probably was supporting one foreign missionary. Two of the five churches did not have to raise money—they simply paid dues. The others needed to have fundraising events.

Phoebe Mann, daughter-in-law of Mary Mann, said, "There were two classes of people in the churches—landowners and sharecroppers. Mary Mann wanted the sharecroppers to come to church. She wanted them to feel a part of it. She often went out into the country in a buggy collecting money for the missionary society. If people did not have money to donate, she would ask if they would like to give a chicken or an egg. Everybody had chickens running around their front yards. Then she would sell them and give the money to the missionary society. In the fall when a hog was killed, she would collect sausage and sell it to the town folks and give the money to the church. That was her business."

85. BROWNSVILLE FUNDRAISING QUILT

Makers: Women of the Brownsville Methodist Circuit. Brownsville, Haywood County, Tennessee, 1937.

Lender: Merikay Waldvogel.

Pieced and embroidered: 78" x 90"; cotton: yellow solid; black cotton embroidery thread; yellow back; no batting; black bias binding; tacked.

The tradition of raising money for worthy projects by inscribing names of donors on the quilt's surface began in the 1800s. Twentieth-century fundraising quilts often had blocks with embroidered names arranged on spokes of a wheel. This quilt's unusual arrangement of names adds to its charm. According to Phoebe Mann, the maker, Mary Mann, did not put batting behind the signatures because she thought it would make the surface "bumpy" and the names could not be read easily.

MAKING LITTLE DO SOMETHING

Reusing Cotton Sacks

A sk a woman about her life in the 1930s and 1940s, and sooner or later you will hear some amusing stories about cotton sacks. Back then, many basic necessities such as flour, corn meal, salt, and sugar were packaged in textile sacks. Tobacco was sold in small cloth pouches. For the farm, fertilizer, animal feed, and cement came in heavy sacks.

When times got tough and cash was in short supply, women of most socioeconomic levels in the cities and the country made dresses, dish towels, table linens, and aprons from sacks. Men wore shirts and even underwear of cotton sack cloth. Middle class homes had window curtains made of sacks, and beds were covered with sheets, pillow cases, and quilts made of sacks. The severe economic conditions had forced everyone into "the same boat," and women found themselves returning to the tradition of recycling what cloth they had.

Women in the South had traditionally "made a little cloth go a long way." In the 1800s, as sacks replaced wooden barrels as the preferred container for meal and flour, women used sack cloth in their quilts. During the War Between the States, women recycled clothing, blankets, and meal sacks to make warm quilts and comforts. In the early 1900s, making quilts and other household items out of feed and flour sacks again became a necessity as women endured world wars and severe economic depressions.

By the mid 1920s, millers' associations and home demonstration agents in the United States were actively promoting

86. Detail of Flour Sack Trademark Quilt (See illustration 90).

creative reuse of flour sacks for clothing and household decorating. Farmers had traditionally returned their empty sacks to the mills, but cleaning and storing the sacks created extra work for the mill workers. So the mill owners began to sell the sacks back to their customers for a few cents, and millers' associations began to print booklets with suggestions for using these cotton sacks.

In the 1920s and early 1930s, sacks were white with trademark emblems in multiple colors. Removing the ink was the first task in converting the sack to a new use. Farm magazines often included ink removal instructions in advice columns written by home economists; and, of course, women shared tips with their friends. If they were unsuccessful in removing the trademark, quiltmakers simply reversed the cloth. Then the trademark did not stand out so clearly. Some women cut around the printed emblem and used the rest of the white cloth for quilt pieces.

When bag manufacturers realized women were using their sacks for sewing projects, they began to print instructions on the sack for removing the ink. However, there was one small problem with a quilt made by Jenny Hall. It had a perfectly white feed sack backing. All the printing was gone except for the three lines of instructions telling how to remove the ink.

87. Bemis Bag Company designed this Ascension Self Rising Flour sack for Pinckneyville Milling Company of Pinckneyville, Illinois. Collection of Anna Cook.

88. Colonial Sugar was packaged in heavy cotton one-hundred-pound sacks. Collection of Anna Cook.

89. Tobacco was also packaged in sacks. Women saved the small cloth sacks to dye for their quilts. Collection of Anna Cook.

1. Revere Sugar sack; *2.* Colonial Sugar sack; *3.* Pied Piper flour sack; *4.* Brown Cow Feed sack with detachable label; *5.* dress made of flour sacks; *6.* apron made from printed flour sack with a border print; *7.* Shawnee's Best Flour sack; *8.* floral print sack fabric; *9.* floral print five-pound flour sack; *10.* five-pound Martha White Flour sack; *11.* Lady Clair Flour sack; *12.* Leo Salt sack; *13.* Jefferson Island salt bag; *14 and 15. Sewing with Cotton Sacks* booklets; *16.* pattern for the dress model is wearing; and *17.* Merit Chicken Feed sack.

   (*Objects are from the collections of Anna Cook, Edna Gossage, Chris Skinker, and the author. Still life arranged by Sue Jenkins and Joyce Gralak.*)

90. FLOUR MILL TRADEMARK QUILT

Maker: Unknown.
  Possibly Murfreesboro, Rutherford County, Tennessee, mid-1930s.

Lender: Hilary Goldstine.

Pieced: 72″ x 88″; white cotton flour sack top with pink and blue sashing; white back; binding is blue straight; embroidery of printed flour trademarks is in pearl cotton thread; cotton batting; quilted in straight lines in sashing and in the background are motifs of spoons, forks, and scissors.

Special thanks go to Rod Kiracofe of San Francisco and to Bonnie Grossman of the Ames Gallery of American Folk Art in Berkeley, California, for providing information.

While some quiltmakers bleached out the flour mill trademarks and others cut them out, this maker chose to use the advertising images in her quilt top design. All the flour mills on the quilt are in Tennessee except two from Kansas. In the upper right hand corner block is a National Recovery Administration (NRA) eagle insignia, which means the quilt was made after 1933 when the NRA was established.

Most women get a twinkle in their eyes and beam with pride when you ask them to relate their "hard times stories" about feed and flour sacks. They freely admit they dressed themselves and their family in used feed, flour, and fertilizer sacks. Most wish they could still buy the cloth and remember it was of much better quality than today's store-bought cloth.

Women sitting around a quilting frame love to tell stories, some of which get a bit risqué. Billy Crumly of Geraldine, Alabama, reconstructed such a story session for a tape recording she calls "Quilt Stories of the 1930s." Several stories are about humorous incidents involving underwear made of sacks. One young girl was out walking with her beau when she tripped and fell. Oh, how embarrassed she was when her betrothed noticed her underdrawers imprinted with the words *Southern Best*! Another story was about a woman who made her husband's drawers from a flour sack and left the words *Self Rising* on the cloth.

Georgia Mize of Sevier County, Tennessee, remembered her mother making her uncle's "step-ins" from Red Cross flour sack cloth. The red cross did not come out in the washing, so her mother centered the red cross across his backside. Georgia said the neighbors always chuckled when they saw his underwear hanging on the clothes line. No wonder these women get a twinkle in their eyes when you ask them about flour sacks.

As competition from the paper bag industry increased, cotton bag manufacturers such as Bemis Bag Company and Werthan Bag Company looked for ways to make their bags more attractive to homemakers. One way was to use cloth imprinted with floral and geometric designs in modernistic colors; a label with the mill trademark was glued to the colorfully printed cloth, thus eliminating the drudgery of removing the ink. Women enthusiastically accepted these new printed sacks. Willie Emert Hogerty told me she went to the James Mill in Knoxville to find a sack that matched cloth she needed to finish a sewing project. She said she walked out of the mill and dumped the chicken feed on the sidewalk. All she wanted was the sack.

I asked Albert Werthan of Werthan Bag Company in Nashville if his company had hired artists to design the geometric and floral prints. He said one woman artist created the designs, and the company set up an in-house intaglio printworks in 1939. The company had sales representatives who visited the local mills on a regular basis.

Bobbie Durrett, owner of the Ringgold Mill near Clarksville, Tennessee, reported that flour trademarks changed often. Salesmen from three bag companies visited him regularly and would help develop the flour trademarks should he decide to purchase bags. His mill had three brands of flour: High Standard, Carnation, and D & F. The High Standard trademark simply had the name in an arc. The D & F trademark featured a young girl handing a biscuit over a fence. The cornmeal bag designed by Bemis Bag Company included the water-powered mill with the dam and covered bridge in the background (See illustration 92). He said the design would be tailored to fit the size of the bag—a larger design for a twenty-five-pound bag than for a ten-pound bag. But when labeled cloth bags were introduced, only one standard size of the trademark was needed.

To encourage the continued interest in cotton sacks, some sack companies actually designed the bags to be sewing projects. For example, sacks designed to become pillow cases were imprinted with delicate floral embroidery motifs. Two bags designed by Percy Kent Bag Company and Chase Bag Company had quilt blocks printed on the sacks (See illustrations 93–96). Other sacks have carried hand puppet and stuffed animal cut-out designs.

The practice of using cotton sacks in sewing projects continued after World War II, but paper was quickly overtaking cloth. By 1949 the paper sack had become the package of choice for bakery flour, but the National Cotton Council with offices in Memphis, Tennessee, continued to encourage the recycling of cotton sacks for household clothing and linens. For instance, as late as 1959 the National Cotton Council teamed up with McCall's Pattern Company to produce a Cotton Bag Loan Wardrobe. Local women's clubs could reserve the collection of women's and children's dresses, choose local models, and produce their own style show. The Cotton Council provided commentary, suggested news releases, and provided idea booklets for cotton bag sewing to be given to the audience.

91. Labelled paisley print White Ring Flour sack designed by Werthan Bag Company in 1950s. Collection of Anna Cook.

92. Covered bridge at Ringgold Mill near Clarksville, Tennessee, in 1910. Photo courtesy of Dr. H. L. Durrett.

Changes in the eating habits of the American family, coupled with a vastly improved system of transportation, led to the demise of many local mills. Those changes and an improved textile industry led to the disappearance of feed and flour sack dresses and quilts. With a renewed interest in 1930s quilts, feed and flour sacks—those with printed trademarks and those with glued labels and figured cloth—are appearing in antique stores and flea markets. Today sacks offer a fascinating subject for discussion with folks who lived through the unusual times of the Great Depression.

93. Heard's Best Flour sack from Raymond Heard Inc., Ruston, Louisiana. Collection of Anna Cook.

94. Back side of Heard's Best Flour sack with printed quilt blocks.

95. Shawnee's Best Flour sack from Shawnee Milling Company of Shawnee, Oklahoma. Collection of Anna Cook.

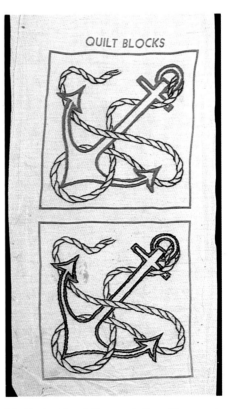

96. Back side of Shawnee's Best Flour sack with printed quilt blocks.

Viola Webb and Her Cotton Sack Quilts

"What I know of my experience, I'm glad to share it with you."
—Viola Webb, age 86.

In the 1930s the Tennessee State Fair had a special category for articles made of recycled cotton sacks. Viola Webb, encouraged by her sister, entered her quilts made from dyed flour sacks. The bags, the thread, and the dye probably cost less than one dollar. She won the first prize of eight dollars in 1934, 1935, and 1937; in some years she also won the second and third prizes.

Her niece, Frances Whittemore, encouraged me to call Viola to set up an interview. So one sunny spring day in 1989, I drove to her farm in Middle Tennessee. Though a mild stroke has restricted her sewing, she still enjoys talking about her special quilts.

Her story is similar to others, but it was so wide ranging that I include it here as an essay on traditional quiltmaking of the 1930s.

MK: Viola, where did you get these sacks? Was there a mill nearby or a general store?

V: No, my sister got them from an institution for ten cents a sack. And they were over a yard—they were one hundred-pound flour sacks. And they are about forty inches long.

MK: So she worked for the institution?

V: No, her husband was a physician there for a long time. She could buy the sacks for ten cents. They had gone through the laundry, but you know they weren't in too good shape—so I washed them a time or two when I got them—and I used a rub board. I sure did. That was rough sailing, too.

MK: Did you have to work hard to get the printing—the trademark—out of the sacks?

V: Yes, sometimes I could bleach it out, but sometimes I'd cut it out. I'd try to get it out somehow. I first dyed the sacks and then I cut them in strips. Here's a bag. I did that years ago—I did that in the early thirties. I've straightened it, you see.

MK: How did you straighten it?

V: I pulled a thread [to find the grain], and then I cut it straight. I dyed them.

MK: What kind of dye did you use?

V: It was Putnam dye—best I can remember. I would boil it out in a kettle well. I'd just boil all the dye into the material I could, and then I'd put a lot of salt in that water and then boil them again until the water's almost clear. So that put the dye into the material. Then I would take my quilt pattern, cut it out, and piece it.

MK: So the backing was also sacks?

V: Yes, it was sacks, too. It wasn't dyed. The lining wasn't dyed. The cotton inside these quilts was raised on this farm. I made batts with cotton cards, and they're all padded with batts that I carded.

MK: I've heard people talk about making cotton batts. How did you do it?

V: You've seen cotton cards, haven't you? Well, instead of making cotton rolls, you make cotton out flat in little batts. I would make just chairfuls. And then I'd prepare to stretch the lining. My frames were hanging from the ceiling. I'd stretch the lining and baste it to the frames which had a lot of holes in them. Then I'd place my batts on the lining and put my quilt top on it. Then I would baste the top to the lining all along the edges of the frame, and then I was ready to quilt.

MK: Tell me about the basting. Did you take big stitches that would go all the way across the quilt or just around the edge?

V: Just around the edges. Because it was stretched tight—the top and bottom, too, was stretched tight on there too. And then with a darning needle I would baste it with the string that came out of the sacks. Instead of pinning it, I used basting thread. I used thread because the pins would get in the way of my arm.

MK: You liked using the sacks? They quilted nice?

V: They quilted good and also those batts. None of these quilts had any of those battings you could buy. They're all cotton.

MK: And they look nice and thin.

V: Well, you could put those batts double and make a heavy quilt, but I didn't like them like that. Now here's a quilt; it's made of sacks, but it's heavier. If I'd had a big family, there wouldn't be a string of these quilts. But I only had one son. So that's how I was able to keep these quilts. Here's some flour sacks I bought years ago.

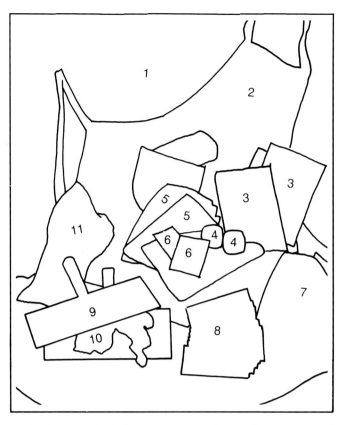

1. Floral print sack cloth; *2.* apron made from sacks; *3.* apron and dress patterns; *4.* boss ball sewing thread; *5.* dyed feed sack cloth; *6.* needle folder; *7.* embroidered bridge table cloth made of sack cloth; *8.* Putnam Dye packages; *9.* cotton cards for making cotton batts for quilt filler; *10.* raw cotton; *11.* a salt sack with black ink trademark.

(Objects are from the collections of Anna Cook, Pauline Pruitt, Eva Earle Kent, and the author. Still life arranged by Sue Jenkins and Joyce Gralak.)

97. Printed flour sacks. Collection of Viola Webb.

MK: Now these are pretty printed flour sacks.

V: I used to make aprons out of them. But when people get their houses burned, I give them away.

MK: Now where would you have got these sacks?

V: At the country store.

MK: Here's a paisley one. (See illustration 97).

V: Sometimes I'd have two just alike.

MK: They do look different from ones in East Tennessee. I just wonder where they came from. You don't have any that still have the labels on them?

V: No, no. They've all been laundered. See here's one that's not be raveled out. It's got a chain stitch along the seam. It is easy to pull out.

MK: Tell me about these quilts that won ribbons. I see there are lots of them. This pink and white one—the Drunkard's Path—did it win a ribbon? (See illustration 99).

V: Yes, now it's faded more than any one I have. It *will* eventually fade, that dye will, red worse to fade than blue.

MK: But you know I like the way it's fading. What color was it?

V: It wasn't this.

MK: So where did you get that pattern—Drunkard's Path?

V: I can't tell you—I might have cut it myself. Now this [looking at the pieces] is easy to cut, but this piece needs to be a little bigger and a seam allowance has to be added. I had a picture. I could see how it was set together. You have to be careful how you place those blocks.

MK: Here's a ribbon that says . . .

V: I can't tell you if the tags are all placed on the right ones.

MK: Tennessee State Fair—First Premium—September 17–22, 1934. This entry tag says Tenn. State Fair, Dept. 6, Entry 3, Class 9–B, Lot 9. That might be a way to trace it—they probably have the records and would be able to say what year.

MK: And then we've got this Robbing Peter to Pay Paul. What do you call it? Orange Peel?

V: That's what my niece called it, but I think the picture said Snowball. But I'm not able to make a snowball out of it.

MK: On this blue and white Robbing Peter to Pay Paul, it says Tennessee State Fair, Dept. 6, Entry 2, Class 9–B, Lot 9. Again, it may not be the right tag for this quilt, and it says Second Prize in 1937. So we have 1934 and 1937.

V: Now that Wedding Ring quilt over there. It's domestic. That's not made from sacks. That's material from dresses. You could buy dress material for eight cents a yard. You could make a dress for eighty-five cents.

MK: So you bought that at one of the little stores down the road?

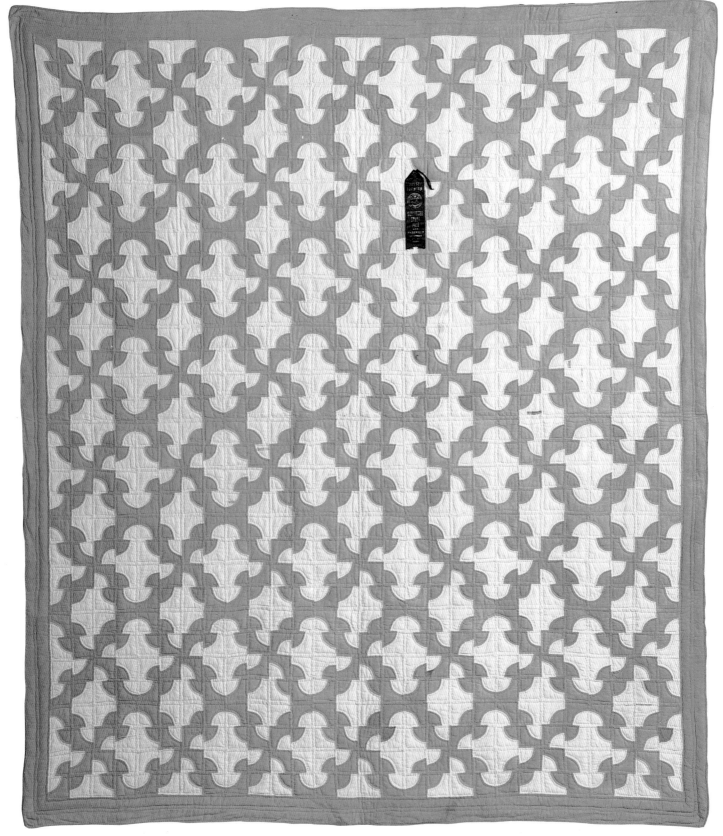

98. DRUNKARD'S PATH

V: Yes, you could buy anything—groceries, hardware, and dress material. Yes, they just had big bolts. They called it brown domestic.

MK: Did you have to wash it before you put it in a quilt?

V: No.

MK: This Basket quilt doesn't look like it's been used or washed (See illustration 102).

V: No, except the sacks have been washed.

MK: The quilting on this is beautiful.

V: This is a little different from the others.

MK: This blue ribbon says September 16–21, 1935. It's a basket. It's got an appliqué handle on it, and then there's also a red ribbon on it which says September 21–26, 1936. It's all sacks also?

V: Yes. And I didn't have any pattern for this. I just looked at a picture. And see I knew this handle had to be bias. And that's what you call feather quilting.

MK: So you basically got your patterns—when you saw a quilt.

V: When I saw a picture. I'd see it, and then I'd go to whittling on it.

MK: Go to whittling on it? I like that.

V: Make me a pattern.

MK: So you cut a pattern?

V: Out of newspaper. And then sandpaper. See the material sticks to the sandpaper—fine sandpaper. I like to press my fabric before I cut my quilt pieces. That's the only way you can get them accurate. Because if there's a wrinkle—why . . .

MK: This Basket also had the homemade batts?

V: Yes. They all had batts made of cotton raised on this farm.

MK: Here's a little bit of print left: T H I F . . .

V: I saw a little bit of print left on one of the linings and I tried to detect what it was, but I never could. It was too dim, too faded. I had washed it.

MK: You know what I noticed when this printing is still on the quilts? The women have reversed them. You know what I mean—the printing is backwards?

V: You know when I made these quilts I never had any idea I'd enter them in the fair or anywhere else. I just made them to wear out.

99. Detail of Drunkard's Path.

Maker: Viola Sanders Webb.
Keltonburg, DeKalb County, Tennessee, mid-1930s.

Lender: Viola Sanders Webb.

Pieced: Cotton flour sacks: pink and white; flour sack back; cotton batting; quilted by the piece in white thread

Viola Webb entered her dyed sack quilts in the Tennessee State Fair for several years during the 1930s. Her quilts regularly won first prize in the category of items made of recycled cotton sacks. This quilt originally was red and white, but the dye has faded to the soft pink it is today.

100. Viola Sanders Webb of Keltonburg, Tennessee, 1989.

MK: You know what I mean—the lettering is on the inside.

V: Yes, I know what you mean.

MK: What is this quilting design supposed to be here? I see some petals and then a grid. Do you remember where you got the quilting design?

V: I just decided what I wanted to do.

MK: It's just beautiful. How did you mark your quilting lines?

V: In times I have marked it with a pencil—lightly, you know. But, well, it's the quilt I gave to my niece. The lady told my sister, "Those pencil marks kindly gives me the creeps." 'Course my niece told me what she said. So the next time I just took my needle and run it just a short distance. I could quilt with that; it'd leave a kind of a print, and that's where I'd quilt.

MK: The amount of quilting on the Basket quilt is just wonderful. And the bindings are on the bias also.

V: Yes, the bindings are on bias. That's the only way you can bind a quilt. You got to be careful—if you do it on machine, the binding walks. For me, I did it all by hand.

MK: Would you have put your backing together by machine?

V: Well, I guess so. I imagine I did.

MK: Did you sew the very edge of the quilt with machine? Some women did that before they put the binding on.

V: I guess I did.

MK: What kind of sewing machine did you use?

V: Here's the machine—the only one I ever bought—bought it in 1928. I've used it all this time.

MK: Is it a treadle machine? Still treadle?

V: Yes.

MK: You've never changed to an electric machine?

V: My son bought me a motor—I didn't like that. I'd rather use my feet.

MK: Is that right? What was the difference?

V: Sometimes I wanted to stop on one stitch. And then when I got that motor started I couldn't stop when I wanted to. With my foot I could. That's the difference.

MK: You had to develop a pretty good rhythm on the treadle machine, didn't you?

V: Yes, I did. Yessir. And it still sews good. And oh, how much it has been used!

MK: Where did you learn how to quilt? Where did you get all these traditions? Or where did you learn how to sew?

V: My mother taught me how to sew. I was about twelve. And nobody enjoyed sewing any more than I did. Ever since I can remember I was holding a needle.

MK: Did she weave?

V: No, she didn't weave. I can't remember ever seeing a loom except in Alabama. I saw them weaving cloth. But my mother had a spinning wheel, and she could spin cotton rolls; you know, make thread, cotton rolls.

MK: So when you were carding the batts for the quilts, it was not unusual?

V: Oh, yes, it was nothing unusual because I learned to do that—I can't even remember learning to do that. And I can't remember learning to quilt either.

V: Here's another, but it's just a string quilt. It's just a top.

MK: And you did it on newspaper?

V: Sears, Roebuck catalog, I guess. You know part of it was soft paper, and it was easier to stitch through. When those quilts was made, times then was hard. Ten cents was hard to get a hold of. My husband had the cattle. We were married in '27—the last of '27. Cattle and, course, the stock market fell. Everything went flat. Couldn't get rid of them. We had spent all of our money buying this farm. He once sold a big red cow and a calf for eight dollars. The cow weighed eight hundred pounds, and the calf weighed two hundred pounds.

MK: Did you rejoice because he sold them, or did you feel bad because the price was so low?

V: Well, we needed some money to pay our taxes and things like that. We didn't need her, and there happened to be a calf with her and all. We had other cows. We milked the cows back then, too, for milk and butter.

MK: You were able to keep the farm?

V: Oh, yes. Still have it. This was . . .

MK: Is it hard talking about it?

V: No, I like telling folks my experiences. I don't feel bad about it. I'm just glad I can live better now than I did then, although I don't know what might happen in the future because I was able to work then.

MK: What did you do?

V: I taught school 'til my son came along. And then I took care of him until he was well along into the grades, and then I went back and taught seven or eight more years.

MK: What did you teach?

V: When I first started, I taught eight grades in a one-teacher school. I didn't think anything about that because I was used to it—a one-teacher school. But I honestly believe they learned more then than they do today in one grade. Anyway, we taught the basics—that's about all we could do. And we tried to teach them morals, and I really was taught morals at home.

MK: During the Depression, did the schools stay open?

V: Yes.

MK: Did you have it rough in the Depression?

V: Yes, but in the country we grew what we needed. Clothing was our problem. In the city, they had it real rough. They had to stand in soup lines and get food out of the garbage. We didn't have it that bad here.

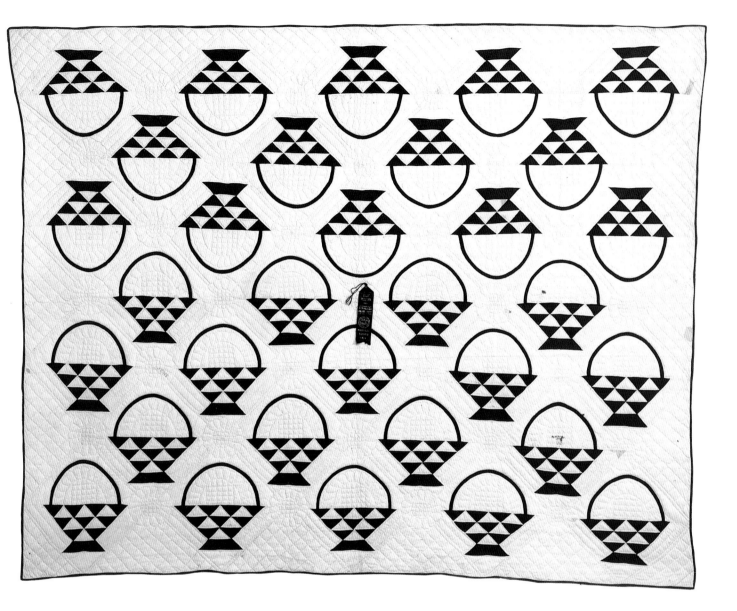

102. BASKET

Maker: Viola Sanders Webb.
  Keltonburg, DeKalb County, Tennessee, mid-1930s.

Lender: Viola Sanders Webb.

Pieced: cotton flour sacks: white and navy; flour sack back; cotton
  batting; decorative floral and straight line quilting throughout the
  quilt.

The Basket Quilt also won a blue ribbon and a prize of eight
dollars at a Tennessee State Fair in the mid-1930s. The materials to
make this quilt cost less than the amount of the prize! The fine
quilting and sewing skills exhibited in this quilt are proof of Viola
Webb's exceptional talents.

101. Detail of Basket.

LOOKING
FOR
BETTER
TIMES

Depression Era Programs

S ometimes history makes more sense when studied outside the formal setting of a classroom. Material culture study, for example, uses objects to get at cultural history. By studying objects, in this case a group of quilts, interviewing the makers, and then going to the library to confirm facts, the researcher often discovers stories left out of history textbooks.

The quilts discussed in this chapter were not made for the specific purposes of warmth and comfort. Instead, they were expressions of quiltmakers coming to grips with the changes the Great Depression brought in their lives. Each quiltmaker was personally affected by innovative social programs of the 1930s. Each quilt story reflects the diversity of groups that tried to soften the effects of the Great Depression.

President Franklin D. Roosevelt's New Deal program carried out by the Civilian Conservation Corps (CCC), the Works Progress Administration (WPA), the National Recovery Administration (NRA), the Resettlement Administration, and, most notably, the Tennessee Valley Authority (TVA), provided hopeful opportunities for sharecroppers, tenant farmers, miners, and textile workers. State public health nurses and home extension agents worked closely with women and children, providing up-to-date information on health and nutrition. And in the mountains, religious and philanthropic groups continued programs aimed at raising the economic standards of families living there.

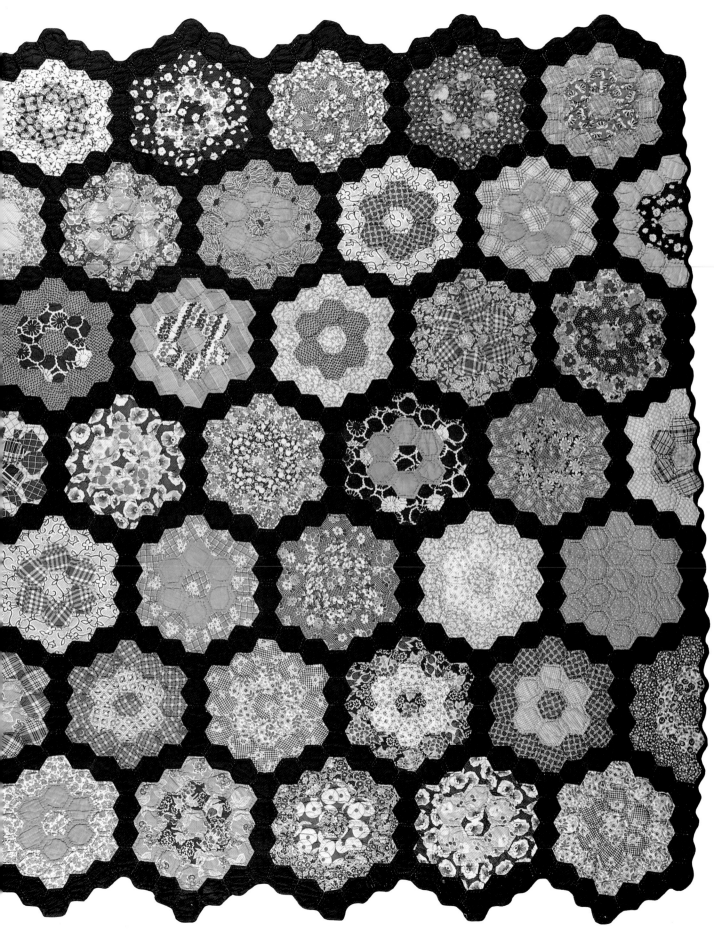

103. Full view of Flower Garden (See illustration 119).

The TVA Quilts

I n 1934 Max Bond was summoned by the officials of the Tennessee Valley Authority to work as a personnel officer with black construction workers at TVA dam sites in northern Alabama along the Tennessee River. Mr. Bond became the highest ranking black man in the agency. He brought with him his wife, Ruth Clement Bond, and their young daughter, Jane. The family chose to move into one of the government-built homes in the racially segregated village.

Ruth Clement Bond's father was a Methodist bishop living in Kentucky. He often spoke out against racial discrimination. Ruth had been raised in an integrated neighborhood and had studied at Northwestern University, receiving a B.A. in English (1925) and an M.A. in English (1930). Prior to coming to TVA with her husband, Ruth had taught high school and college English for five years in Kentucky State College.

When Ruth moved to the segregated Wheeler Dam construction village, she became fascinated with the traditional ways of the women living there. "I decided I could learn from the women and they could learn from me," she reported in a 1989 interview. Ruth said the women were wall-papering their houses with pages from Sears catalogs because that was what they had on hand. She suggested they have a TVA room in their houses—not necessarily the living room—and she encouraged them to use indigenous products.

She and her husband had a local man make furniture for their own house from the willow trees in the area. When the other families liked the furniture and asked about it, the Bonds encouraged them to decorate their homes using inexpensive materials on hand.

The women under Ruth Bond's direction used flour sacks stored in the bunkhouse warehouse for such things as curtains and linens. They used corn shuck rugs dyed with local herbs for floor coverings. She recalled, "We were making little do something."

Ruth Bond began to travel regularly to the several black construction villages around the area when the women got together for quiltings. The women were making quilts from the popular patterns of the day, and Ruth Bond came up with the idea of making a pattern for a TVA quilt that represented the power that electricity would bring into their lives. She then drew on brown paper a full length black figure holding in his hands a bolt of lightning. She called it simply "TVA Quilt." Several women decided to make that quilt, which soon became known as the "Black Power Quilt" and took on added significance.

Rose Thomas and her husband, who was Max Bond's assistant, were living at a Pickwick Dam construction village. The women used to gather in each other's cottages to do

Ruth Clement Bond

Ruth Clement Bond is a human rights activist whose life is a reflection of her beliefs. She was born into the family of Bishop George C. Clement, who was co-chairman of the Inter-racial Commission of the Federal Council of Churches and whose wife, Emma (the mother of seven children) became the first Black woman to be named American Mother of the Year.

Ruth learned early the rewards of sharing and of working with others, regardless of race and nationality. Raised in Louisville, Kentucky, she went to Livingstone College and then to Northwestern University, from which she received B.A. and M.A. degrees in English and sociology. She was head of the English Department on three continents: Kentucky State University, L'Ecole Normale de Martissant in Haiti, and the University of Liberia, of which her husband was president.

For twenty years, Ruth Bond accompanied her husband, Dr. J. Max Bond, first to Haiti and then to several African and Asian countries where she worked closely with the women.

In 1966 the Bonds returned to the United States and settled in Washington, D.C. Since their return, she has served with a variety of women's groups dealing with human rights. At present, she is involved in the International Committee of the Red Cross and the Boys' and Girls' Clubs of Greater Washington.

Her faith in education is reflected through her three children: Jane Bond Howard, Ph.D., Professor of European History, Lincoln University; J. Max Bond, Jr., Dean of School of Architecture, City College of New York; and George Clement Bond, Ph.D., Professor of Anthropology, Teachers' College, Columbia University.

105. Detail of Lazy Man.

104. LAZY MAN

Maker: Grace Reynolds Tyler.
   Wheeler Dam Village, Northern Alabama, 1934.

Designer: Ruth Clement Bond.

Owner: Grace Reynolds Tyler.

Pieced and appliqué: 65″ x 81″; cotton: solid colors; orange cotton
   back; cotton batting; circular quilting in border and diamond
   quilting in central medallion using brown thread.

The wives of black construction workers at the Tennessee Valley
Authority (TVA) dam project in North Alabama often met to do
needlework and socialize. Ruth Clement Bond, whose husband was
the highest ranking black official at TVA, met with these women.
She was fascinated by the local crafts, especially quiltmaking. She
developed this appliqué design that Grace Tyler and at least three
other women used in their quilts.

needlework: sewing, crochet, knitting, and quiltmaking. When Ruth Bond brought her quilt designs to them, Rose decided to make a quilt. As it turned out, it was her first and last quilt. It is the same design used by Grace Tyler (See illustration 104).

I asked Rose why she liked her quilt so much. She said, "It tells the story of what was happening for the black man on the TVA dam construction sites. The women were excited about the new opportunities, and they wanted to show them in their quilt designs."

I asked her to tell me what the different parts of the appliqué picture meant. She said, "The man with his banjo is full of frivolity. He is between the hand of the government [TVA] and the hand of a woman. He must choose between the government job and the life he has known."

I asked her if the woman whose form is just visible off to the right of the man is his mother or a girlfriend. "Oh, it is definitely a girlfriend," she answered.

What is the viewer to think about his choice? Rose replied, "We wanted to show that he chose the TVA job. It has a hopeful message."

Grace Tyler liked the pattern immediately. She said, "I was always doing that. I'd see a pattern I liked, and then I'd go home and draw it from memory. I made lots of my quilts like that." She called her pattern Lazy Man (See illustration 104).

When asked about the significance of the pattern of the quilt, Ruth Bond, the designer, simply said it was a positive message of the black man's part in the rebirth and growth of the economy. "Things were getting better, and the black worker had a part in it."

When asked about the white hand extending from a uniform sleeve reaching in from outside the picture, she at first could not see it and did not remember it. Then she added: "It represents the black man moving away from the hand of the law. In spite of the law, he is moving to become indepen-

106. Ruth Bond's husband, J. Max Bond, organized a health clinic for the mothers of small children whose fathers were building dams for TVA. Jane Bond, young daughter of Max and Ruth Bond, is second from right on the first row. Photo courtesy of Ruth Clement Bond.

107. Appliqué Tennessee Valley Authority quilt design of a black fist. Cotton: 11¼" x 13"; unquilted. Designed by Ruth Clement Bond, 1934. Made by Rose Marie Thomas.

dent and to become an important part of society." She did not see it as the white hand of the law controlling the black man.

Rose Thomas made three small cloth appliqué blocks using Ruth Bond's TVA quilt designs. (See illustrations 107–109), one of which is of the man with the musical instrument. Another one depicts a man on a crane digging out earth for a TVA dam. The third is of a black fist clenching tightly a red lightning bolt. I asked her to discuss the meaning of that quilt design: "We were pushing up through obstacles—through objections. We were coming up out of the Depression, and we were going to live a better life through *our* efforts. The opposition wasn't going to stop us."

After she finished her Lazy Man quilt, Grace Tyler made another quilt using a Ruth Bond design. It was one of her favorites. She described it as a giant black fist holding a lightning bolt. In 1934 her husband went to the nearby TVA offices at Muscle Shoals for a meeting and took the Fist quilt to show some visiting dignitaries. To her dismay, Grace's husband returned that night without the quilt; he had given it to one of the dignitaries. She has grieved over the loss of that quilt for more than fifty years, and because of that she decided not to lend her Lazy Man quilt to the exhibit which accompanies this book. I suspected that the Black Fist appliqué block owned by Rose Thomas was the same design Grace used for her Fist quilt. When I showed her a photograph, she assured me it was.

Ruth Bond took with her one of the quilts in her original Black Power design when she left the Wheeler Dam area. Now it, too, is missing. Apparently it was stolen from the Bonds' household goods stored in an Atlanta warehouse. She described it as having a full length appliqué black figure with a bolt of lightning that extends across the man's body from one upraised fist to the other fist. Recently, from her home in Washington, DC, Ruth tried to locate a Black Power quilt to replace her stolen one but was unsuccessful. Rose

109. Appliqué Tennessee Valley Authority quilt design of man with crane. Cotton: 13¾" x 17½"; unquilted. Designed by Ruth Clement Bond, 1934. Made by Rose Marie Thomas.

108. Appliqué Tennessee Valley Authority quilt design of man with musical instrument. Cotton: 13½" x 17½"; unquilted. Designed by Ruth Clement Bond, 1934. Made by Rose Marie Thomas.

Thomas gave Ruth Bond her TVA quilt, which Ruth has loaned to the travelling exhibit.[2]

Ruth Bond still believes that "the threshold of understanding is raised through participation in new cultural approaches. That is what I was doing at Wheeler Dam." She has worked in similar capacities in other women's programs in Haiti, Liberia, Afghanistan, Tunisia, Sierre Leone, and Malawi. Today she serves on boards of various community and international organization in the Washington, D.C. area.

Jane Bond-Howard, daughter of Ruth and Max Bond, added, "My parents were the conveyors between the general white population and the black population. They were the hyphen between the two groups. In the 1930s, we didn't have mass culture brought into the homes through television. Many people like my parents brought that to black families. Historians need to study people like my parents—the children of black educators and ministers of the early twentieth century."

Although Ruth Bond was not trained in the fine arts, she showed artistic talent in portrait drawing and ceramics. The large silhouette figures in the Lazy Man quilt have elements in common with the work of Aaron Douglas, a Harlem Renaissance painter who worked at Fisk University in Nashville in 1934. But Ruth is quick to point out that the work of French artist Henri Matisse also has similar human figures. Aaron Douglas was known for his murals and illustrations in such books as God's Trombones by James Weldon Johnson. Ruth cannot remember using the work of Aaron Douglas as in-spiration for her designs, but she admits the man with the banjo does have certain Douglasesque elements. The large hard-edged figure in silhouette with slits to mark the eye region and the leaves that look like palms appear often in the work of Aaron Douglas. Ruth feels that those types of images were common in Depression art and might have served as inspiration for her designs.

These TVA quilt images, so reminiscent of WPA mural art, stand in stark contrast to popular quilts of the 1930s. Ruth Bond developed these nontraditional designs hoping to "break through ignorance." She did not specify whose ignorance or of what kind. That is the reason why the quilt designs are of historical and social interest today. They reflect social changes, and they reflect hope. To those of us who know what has occurred in the years following the Depression, the appliqué images are strong, almost shocking. They are made even more so appearing unexpectedly on the soft surface of a quilt. In one sense, they are naive. Yes, TVA was providing new opportunities for black workers in the area, but at the same time it was perpetuating the long-held custom of segregation.

Ruth Bond was excited about the future; after all, TVA was giving paying jobs to black sharecroppers. For many of the men, it was the first cash they had ever earned; for their wives, it was the first leisure time they had had. The women enthusiastically accepted Ruth Bond's quilt designs and made them into quilts that represented their feelings of hope for the future.

110. Home of a Baptist preacher in northern Alabama, 1934. Photo courtesy of Ruth Clement Bond.

111. Boy of ten plowing in northern Alabama in 1934. Photo courtesy of Ruth Clement Bond.

Aunt Lizzie's Arrowcraft Quilt

I n 1910 the alumnae of Pi Beta Phi fraternity voted to establish a Settlement School to honor the founders of the fraternity. They chose the Appalachian Mountain region, which they were told was sorely in need of educational facilities. A committee was dispatched to find a "suitable site for the erection of an independent settlement school in which special emphasis was to be laid upon industrial features."[2]

Because the State of Tennessee lacked sufficient tax revenues in sparsely populated areas, private support of its public schools was encouraged. On visiting a one-room school in the mountains near Gatlinburg, the fraternity's president remarked: "All the children were dressed in calico and were barefooted, but had bright intelligent faces, and they were clean. The trouble with the schools seems to be that few of the teachers have ever gone to a high school, and that they are teaching the same grade work they have done themselves."[3]

On January 20, 1912, Martha Hill of Nashville was hired to teach at the settlement school for three months at a salary of forty dollars per month. The first session opened in March with fourteen pupils. Three months later, thirty-three pupils were enrolled. Two years later when the school closed for the summer, 158 students were enrolled.

In March 1915, Miss Pollard, director of the school, wrote to *The Arrow*, the fraternity's national newsletter: "We are hoping to emphasize the industrial side of our work more and more. We are hoping to start basket making in the school, hoping that it will prove a profitable industry. Many of the women make exquisite patchwork quilts, and some will make the hand woven coverlids and blankets. If a sale could be found for these articles, many might undertake the work."[4] No doubt, she was hoping the Pi Beta Phi alumnae chapters across the country would sell these handicrafts; and, since 1915, Pi Beta Phi chapters have sold millions of these products—through the Arrowcraft Shop.

In 1934 when the Great Smoky Mountains National Park opened, Gatlinburg changed forever. The value of land skyrocketed as facilities were built to accommodate the increasing number of tourists. In 1945 the Fraternity established the Summer Craft Workshop in conjunction with the University of Tennessee. In 1970 the name was changed to Arrowmont School of Arts and Crafts.

Today the Pi Beta Phi Elementary School is supported by tax dollars. Arrowcraft Shop staff work with area women who make woven items and handmade crafts to sell to Pi Beta Phi alumnae and to tourists who visit Gatlinburg. The Arrowmont School of Arts and Crafts continues to be a leader in innovative art and craft education for all ages.

Not every philanthropic venture in the Appalachian Mountains has been so successful. Credit must go to the early supporters, but also to mountain people such as "Aunt Lizzie" Reagan who shared their knowledge of traditional crafts.

112. Elizabeth Cogdill Reagan, known as "Aunt Lizzie" Reagan. Photo taken in 1930s by Doris Ullmann. Photo courtesy of LaDelle Reagan Compton.

Aunt Lizzie Reagan died in 1946 leaving a trunk to her granddaughter. In the bottom of the trunk was a string quilt made of scraps of cloth woven at Arrowcraft (See illustration 113). By using those scraps in the quilt, she has left for others a historical document. By studying the history of the school, one cannot miss this strong mountain woman's presence.

This is her story. In 1918, at the age of sixty, Elizabeth Cogdill Reagan went to work as a babysitter for the infant son of a couple who worked at the school. She was known by all as "Aunt Lizzie." She had raised five children of her own and was living alone in a mountain cabin. At the school she soon became a very important staff member. She served not only as a link between the mountain people and the school but also as a link to the nineteenth-century way of life when women wove cloth for their families.

Aunt Lizzie knew everyone for miles around and their family histories. When the nurse came to the school, she took few long trips without first consulting Aunt Lizzie about direction, roads, and family. She was on the school staff for nine years.

After nine years, when she "retired" to her cabin on the side of a mountain, she still kept a garden and had her pet cow. When the school bought a big, old-fashioned loom, she returned to help the staff thread it. "After thirty-five years away from a loom, Aunt Lizzie set up the loom, put on a warp, and threaded it. Not a single thing had she forgotten in all that time. In fact, she knew many a little turn that the weaving teacher had never heard of, and Aunt Lizzie told her with great pride."[5]

In appreciation of all that Aunt Lizzie had done and had meant to the school, the settlement school committee presented her with a Pi Beta Phi Patroness pin.

113. ARROWCRAFT WEAVING QUILT

Maker: Aunt Lizzie Reagan.
Gatlinburg, Sevier County, Tennessee, 1930s.

Lender: La Delle Reagan Compton, granddaughter.

Crazy Patch: 70″ x 79″; cotton and wool; blue and brown striped and checked handwoven swatches; plaid flannel back; no batting; edge has back turned to front by machine; unquilted; special surface techniques include briar stitching over seams.

In the early part of the twentieth century Pi Beta Phi established a settlement school in Gatlinburg to educate mountain children. Finding success with the school children, the staff set up the Arrowcraft workshop for the parents. Brooms, baskets, and woven goods were sold throughout the country bringing much needed income to the people of Gatlinburg. A mountain woman named Aunt Lizzie Reagan (1858–1946) worked first as a housekeeper and babysitter at the teachers' cottage, but she was most valuable as a weaver and as a liaison between the school and the community people. Sometime in the 1930s she made this quilt of scraps from Arrowcraft weaving projects. Today it is a record of early weaving at Arrowcraft.

114. Detail of Arrowcraft.

"Getting the Blue Eagle Pulled"

Edna Gossage began to tell a story about a set of appliqué quilt blocks made of sugar sack cloth given to her by fellow union members at the Harriman Hosiery Mill in Harriman, Tennessee. She said the workers had made raffle quilts to raise money for their strike efforts, but these blocks of different flowers were given to her to thank her for her efforts on their behalf in getting "the blue eagle pulled." When asked what "the blue eagle" was and how it could be "pulled," she smiled. "The blue eagle was a very familiar insignia printed on product advertisements and package labels in 1933 and 1934."

She explained that when Franklin Roosevelt became president, one of his earliest pieces of legislation was the National Industrial Recovery Act. Company owners agreed to abide by a set of liberalized work rules which included allowing workers to organize or join a union. At first, the legislation was very popular, and companies were proud to display the blue eagle, the insignia of the National Recovery Administration (NRA); but within a short while, it declined in popularity. In 1935 the United States Supreme Court declared the legislation unconstitutional.

The Harriman Hosiery Mill signed the rules of conduct, but it did not follow the rules. In October 1933, the company fired 56 workers when more than 650 had joined a union. Edna's husband was one of the laid-off workers, and she and her husband, along with others, began a six-month campaign to get the "blue eagle pulled" at Harriman Hosiery Mill. It took many trips to Washington. The workers eventually won a favorable ruling; but the company appealed, thereby delaying action. Finally, in April 1934, they succeeded in getting the blue eagle pulled.

When a company signed on, it agreed not to do business with non-NRA companies. Soon carloads of returned merchandise produced by Harriman Hosiery Mill began piling up at the company's doors. Neither Edna nor her husband felt like returning to the mill to work. They had applied for a home through the Resettlement Administration at Cumberland Homesteads near Crossville and had been accepted.

116. Friendship quilt block made for Edna Gossage in appreciation of her efforts to help her local garment workers union.

117. The National Recovery Administration blue eagle appeared on goods produced by companies who had a signed workers' rights compact developed by President Roosevelt in 1933. In 1935 the United States Supreme Court declared it unconstitutional.

115. Edna Gossage of Cumberland Homesteads near Crossville, Tennessee, 1989.

The Cumberland Homesteads

118. Edna Gossage, with husband Roy and son Roy, Jr., stands beside barn they lived in while their house at Cumberland Homesteads near Crossville, Tennessee, was being built. Photo courtesy of Edna Gossage.

On July 8, 1934 (three days after Mrs. Eleanor Roosevelt made a visit), Edna Gossage and her family moved to Cumberland Homesteads. As the self-appointed historian of Cumberland Homesteads, she has spent fifteen years gathering factual information about this innovative program begun in the early 1930s. She hopes one day to publish a book about her findings.

She said thousands of people applied for the 250 spaces in the Cumberland Homesteads program. All the homesteaders were interviewed and their backgrounds checked. At first her family was not accepted because her husband had been in jail as a result of his union activities, but the manager of Cumberland Homesteads at the time overruled the investigators and said, "They're leaders—they're the kind we want."

According to Edna Gossage, county agent Bob Lyons had proposed the original idea of a homestead program in the Cumberland area. It was one of 101 similar projects set up by the federal government around the country to give people a new chance by providing a piece of land and a house. Mrs. Roosevelt was especially interested in the homestead programs and visited them often. Mr. Lyons felt a subsistence program of this type was even better than a road building program because the people were working to build something together. He felt it would provide more hope than a make-work program.

When a family was accepted in the Homesteads, usually the man arrived first and was given a job based on his skills. He did not necessarily work on his own house, but two-thirds of his wages went to pay off his debts to the program. Families first moved into one of the barns with other newcomers. As their homes were finished, they moved out of the barns.

Other cooperative programs were set up so that families could meet their payments. For example, homesteaders were paid one-third in cash and the other two-thirds in credit hours for crops they grew. There was also a cannery, a trading post, and a gift shop run co-operatively.

Cumberland Homesteads was considered a showplace of the New Deal, with reporters from all over the world coming to visit. Cumberland homesteaders eventually bought their own homes, and they were able to maintain a strong sense of community. Homestead projects in other parts of the country were sold to private concerns.

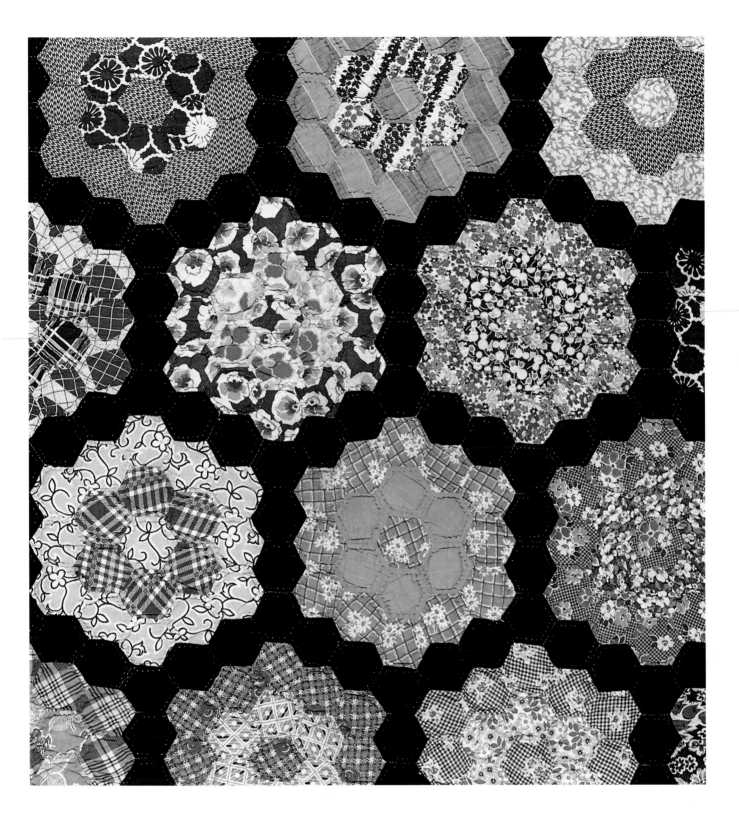

119. FLOWER GARDEN

Makers: Effie Johnson and Reba Johnson Parham.
 Cumberland Homesteads, Cumberland County, Tennessee, 1938.

Lender: Reba Johnson Parham.

Pieced: 67″ x 84″; cotton: black solid and various calico prints;
 white heavy cotton back; black bias binding; cotton batting;
 quilted by the piece in white thread.

The Flower Garden quilt was one of the most popular quilt
patterns in the 1930s. Most were made with pastel colors. This one
using black is distinctive. By 1938, the maker's family was settled
into a new home surrounded by productive farm land near
Crossville at the Cumberland Homesteads.

Turkey Oak Club

Turkey Oak Club of Cumberland Homesteads was one of the women's clubs organized by Marie Irwin, the local home economist. At the monthly meeting, Marie Irwin gave demonstrations about new home products and garden crops. She also gave lectures on nutrition and health. Tuberculosis was the main concern, and nurse Amy Cox often came to do screenings of children at the group's meeting.

Marie Irwin, the home economist for Cumberland Homesteads, was affiliated with a Friends organization concerned with people in Appalachia. Under her leadership, women's groups that met regularly were established. She taught home management, child care, health, and crafts: she saw quiltings as a good way for women to get to know one another. Mrs. Irwin also set up a loom house. The government furnished six-heddle looms, table looms, and two instructors; and the women sold their items at the gift shop. Edna Gossage said she once wove enough wool fabric for a man's suit. She also wove a rug to specifications sent by a woman in Iowa.

Most families owed the United States government an average of $2,365 to be paid off in twenty years. The bookkeeping arrangements were never clear; and when federal comptrollers came in to check, they declared the procedures illegal. Edna recalled, "The early managers were just trying to do the best job they could to carry out the dream." In the 1940s several families were taken to court for not paying the money they owed. Most of them felt the rules for payment had been changed in the middle of the game.

Edna said, "It is remarkable Cumberland Homesteads is still in such good shape. We were stubborn mountain people, and we had common sense. We didn't go along with all the hair-brained government ideas." Edna's husband was paid sixty cents per hour—one-third in cash and two-thirds toward the home and the stock in the community. Edna taught in the first school. The government wanted to assign a teacher who could get paid on the Homestead budget—on credit. Later Edna worked for Save the Children Federation

and New Youth Administration distributing clothes donated by people in urban areas. She was paid sixty dollars per month, but this ended with Pearl Harbor.

Edna's other accomplishments include starting the Daniel Arthur Rehabilitation Center in her home in Clinton, being an actress at Cumberland County Playhouse, and working for the Tennessee Department of Public Welfare for twenty-eight years.

Although most of the homesteaders had to leave the area to make some money, many kept their houses. Reba Johnson Parham's father worked in the sawmill at the Homesteads, but in 1941 went to work on the Panama Canal for two years. The money he earned there paid off the Cumberland Homesteads farm. Their farm was about thirty-six acres and cost $2,000 for the house and land.

Edna Gossage's family moved to Oak Ridge and then Clinton where they worked for the government for five years during the 1940s. They kept their property at Cumberland Homesteads, even when the government tried to take it, claiming it was abandoned.

Today the community is much like it was fifty-five years ago. The approximately 250 houses made of the local coral-colored crab orchard stone sit on shaded plots of land averaging sixteen acres. The area is as picturesque as when it was first envisioned, but economic development has come and gone. Today its hope lies in tourism developed at nearby retirement villages. Nearby Cumberland State Park was built in 1938–1939 by the Civilian Conservation Corps (CCC).

120. Typical Cumberland Homesteads house built of local Crab Orchard stone. Photo from the Library of Congress.

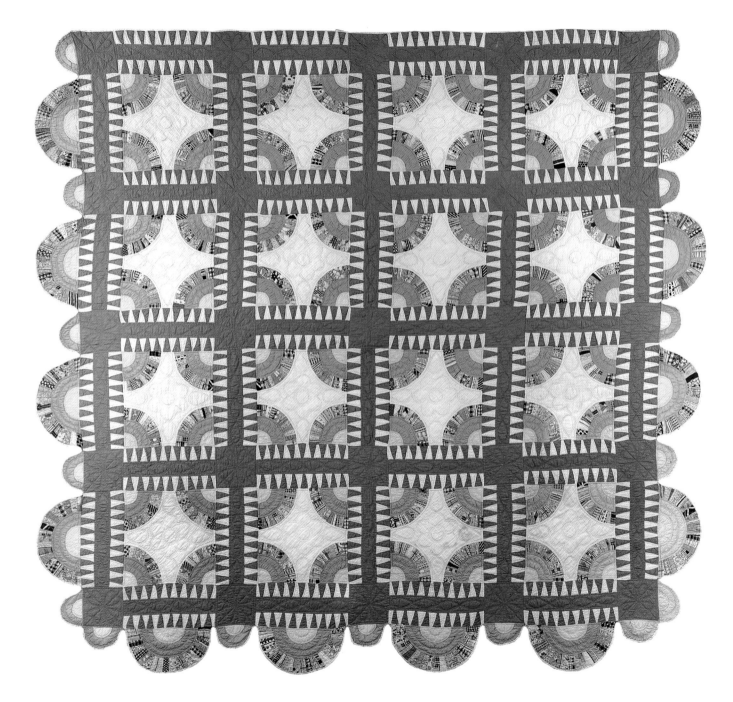

121. Full view of New York Beauty (See illustration 30).

CONCLUSION

When I walked into that antique store in 1974, I was looking for symbols of comfort, warmth, and security. I thought I was unique, but in reality I was being subtly swept up in a national wave of nostalgia similar to one that occurred in the 1920s. Affluent women living in urban areas in that decade no doubt felt the same longing for simpler times. My decorating choices, and those of 1920s women, had been subtly affected by the times—and more probably by marketing directors attuned to the national consciousness of large groups of consumers.

I cannot say I regret being "drawn" to that quilt; and although I cannot speak for the thousands of 1920s and 1930s quiltmakers, I suspect they gained enormous pleasure from their quiltmaking experiences.

Quilt designers and marketers would not have been so successful in changing quilt styles had the quiltmakers of the 1930s not found their products and patterns appropriate and appealing. With family spending drastically reduced to the basic essentials—food, shelter, and clothing—sewing, including quiltmaking, continued as a viable, pleasing, and productive activity. Entrepreneurs large and small, fighting fiercely for a share of this market, produced fabric and innovations that changed traditional quilt styles. Thus do 1930s quilts reflect their times.

When I began this research, I wanted to look for unique Depression Era quilts but was encouraged instead to look at typical Depression Era quilts—ones made of pastel-colored cloth in patterns called Double Wedding Ring, Grandmother's Flower Garden, and so forth. I wanted to know why Depression Era quilts generally were pretty and were much the same all over the country.

Due to improved, low-cost media forms such as the newspaper, magazine, and mail order catalog, even the most remote farm family had access to the great national marketplace. Improved mail systems using improved highways and railroads brought the same type of fabric and quilt patterns quickly and inexpensively to women in all regions of the country. Editors of magazines and newspapers discovered that needlework patterns and quilt patterns sold magazines and newspapers, and the marketplace needed to be replenished frequently to maintain the public's interest in consumer products. Designers suddenly found themselves in demand. Due to the increased interest, thousands of new or updated quilt patterns entered the market.

These new patterns, made up in designer pastel colors, trickled down to the old time quiltmakers—the "authentic" quiltmakers, as I call them. The soft pastel quilts became the models for 1930s quilts made throughout the country; and by dyeing white flour sacks, women were able to have cheap pastel cloth. When sack companies began to produce sacks in the same pretty pastel prints available in general stores, women with very little cash could produce quilts like those in magazines.

What is interesting, but not unusual when you stop to think about it, is that if you read magazines of the 1920s and 1930s—especially women's magazines—you would never know the country was experiencing an economic depression. People do not want to read about hard times; they do not want to be reminded of them. Obviously, products do not sell when associated with hard times. This marketing maxim is probably the reason Depression Era quilts suddenly changed so radically and why they appear to be soft covers for hard times.

The Depression Era quilt became so prevalent that it became the epitome of American quilt design. For many, it was the only quilt style they knew. In the Quilts of Tennessee survey, for instance, it was not unusual for a quilt owner to say that his or her Flower Garden quilt in pastel colors was over one hundred years old.

In the frenzy of the Quilt Revival of the 1920s and 1930s, traditional quiltmaking was romanticized. Recent quilt research, especially that published by the American Quilt Study Group, aims to set the story straight. Most research has concentrated on nineteenth-century quiltmaking, but I encourage others to look beneath the soft covers of twentieth-century quilts. One obvious advantage is that many of the quiltmakers are still living. Another is that collections of magazines, farm journals, and newspapers are readily available in local and university libraries.

In the course of this research, I have often felt like a private detective tracking down people and quilts, then writing down the stories. As I write this conclusion, I think of the questions for which I still seek answers. I mention them here in the hopes that someone else will also be inclined to investigate them.

Who are the unattributed traditional quiltmakers who might have developed patterns for the commercial quilt designers?

Where are the Anne Orr quilts that appear as completed quilts in her magazine articles? How successful was the Orr Studio? How many quilt patterns were sold nationally? How many women were employed?

Where is the grand prize-winning quilt of the Sears National Quilt Contest? Where are other local and regional winning quilts? Where is Mr. Frenchy Cottrell, a resident of Nashville in 1933? He is the only male quiltmaker known to have won a prize in the Sears National Quilt Contest.

Where is Grace Tyler's Fist quilt, the one her husband gave to a visiting dignitary without her permission? Where is Ruth Bond's Black Power quilt, the one given to her as a gift and later stolen from her household belongings stored in an Atlanta warehouse?

I also raise one issue for consideration. Are quilts art? Early twentieth-century quilt designers, especially Marie Webster, Rose Kretsinger, and Anne Orr, are credited with raising the quilt from a folk art form to a fine art form. If a quilt is fine art, does it continue to be so when duplicated hundreds of times? And who deserves credit for these duplicates—the designer or the maker? Of course, this problem only arises in cases of contests, exhibits, or books such as this one. It obviously was not an issue at the Sears National Quilt Contest where women submitted quilts made from commercial patterns and won prizes.

In short, the period of 1920 through 1940 is a rich era for research. It is a story of a long-standing traditional skill being rediscovered and transformed by people outside the circle of traditional quiltmakers. Gained were thousands of new quiltmakers making thousands of new quilts. Lost were regional traditional quilt forms and practices. In their place was a homogenized quilt form, and a soft cover which on the surface does not reflect the hard times of the Great Depression but, in fact, does reflect the complex forces changing forever the lives of American families.

Correspondence may
be directed to:

Merikay Waldvogel
1501 Whitower Road
Knoxville, TN 37919

NOTES

Quilt Revival

1. Marie Webster, *Quilts: Their Story and How to Make Them* (New York: Doubleday, Page and Company, 1915), xvi.
2. Carrie A. Hall and Rose G. Kretsinger, *The Romance of the Patchwork Quilit in America* (New York: Bonanza Books, 1935), 241.
3. Advertisement, *Knoxville News-Sentinel,* March 12, 1933, 3.
4. *Sears Century of Progress in Quilt Making* (Chicago: Sears, Roebuck and Company, 1934), 6.
5. Lena Davis, letter to Mrs. Murray, March 13, 1933, in collection of the Rose Center and Council for the Arts, Morristown, Tennessee.
6. *Needlecraft Magazine* (fragment), in Huff Family Collection.
7. Frederick Herrschner Company, *Fall and Winter Catalogue 1932–1933* (fragment), in Huff Family Collection.
8. Anne Orr, "Needlework," *Good Housekeeping,* January 1938, 60.
9. "Ann's Scrap Quilt," Laura Wheeler Pattern Number 600, in Huff Family Collection.
10. Florence La Ganke, "Nancy Page Quilt Club," *Nashville Banner,* May 21, 1933, 15.
11. H. VerMehren, *Colonial Quilts* (Des Moines: H. Ver Mehren, 1933), 3.

Refining the Tradition

1. *Quilter's Hall of Fame* (Vienna, Virginia: The Continental Quilting Congress, Inc., 1980), 4.
2. Jean Dubois, "Anne Orr—She Captured Beauty," *Quilter's Newsletter Magazine,* 12; "Gifted Nashville Artist the Designer of Twelve Best Selling Books of Art Needlework," *Nashville Banner,* June 23, 1917, 6.
3. Anne Orr, *Filet Crochet Designs and Their Appropriate Uses,* Book 29, rev. ed. (Nashville: Orr Studio), 1. Found in *Anne Orr's Book of Stitches and Designs,* in Tennessee State Library and Archives.
4. Gedy Higgins, telephone interview with the author October 2, 1989.
5. Anne Orr, "A Christmas Forethought," *Good Housekeeping,* November 1919, 69.
6. Anne Orr, "Anne Orr's Needlework," *Good Housekeeping,* January 1925, 64–65.
7. Cuesta Benberry, letter to the author, August 17, 1989.
8. Anne Orr, "Quilt Making of Today," *Good Housekeeping,* January 1935, 56–57.
9. Anne Orr, "Enchanting for Chaise Lounge or Bed," *Good Housekeeping,* February 1936, 58–59.
10. Anne Orr, "Pieced and Appliqued Quilts and Spreads," *Good Housekeeping,* January 1934, 55.
11. Anne Orr, "Quilt Making in Old and New Designs," *Good Housekeeping,* January 1933, 56.
12. Anne Orr, "Everybody's Doing Needlework!" *Good Housekeeping,* January 1939, 61.

13. Anne Orr, "Needlework!" *Good Housekeeping,* January 1938, 61.
14. Anne Orr, "Anne Orr's Suggestions for Period Decoration," *Good Housekeeping,* January 1930, 77.
15. Anne Orr, "New Quilts with Rugs to Match," *Good Housekeeping,* January 1932, 104.
16. *Sears Century of Progress in Quilt Making,* (Chicago: Sears, Roebuck and Company, 1934), 18.
17. John Rice Irwin, *A People and Their Quilts* (Exton, Pennsylvania: Schiffer Publishing Company, 1983), 70, 82.
18. Euretha Irwin, interview with author, September 6, 1989.
19. Cuesta Benberry, conversation with author, March 18, 1989.
20. Andrena Phillips, telephone interview with author, October 3, 1989.

Sears National Quilt Contest

1. Sears, Roebuck and Company, *Sears, Roebuck and Company Catalog,* Spring 1933.
2. Ida M. Stow, letter to Sears, Roebuck and Company, June 6, 1933, in *Quilter's Journal,* July 1985, 13.
3. Advertisement, *Nashville Banner,* May 21, 1933, 16.
4. Claire Gilbert, telephone interview with author, June 26, 1989.
5. Mainer Lee Toler, "Eleven Hundred Handmade Quilts on Display at Sears-Roebuck Co.," *Atlanta Constitution,* May 28, 1933, 4M.
6. Ibid, 4M.
7. Advertisement, *Atlanta Constitution,* June 1, 1933.
8. Louise Edelman, telephone interview with author, June 27, 1989.
9. Advertisement, *Nashville Tennessean,* May 21, 1933, 5.
10. Anne Orr, "The Winners of Our Quilt Contest," *Good Housekeeping,* August 1939, 61.

Looking for Better Times

1. Although Rose Thomas's TVA Quilt is not pictured in this book, it is included in the traveling exhibit. It is exactly the same pattern as Grace Tyler's Lazy Man quilt (See illustration 104), which will not be in exhibit.
2. Jean Orr Donaldson, *A Century of Friendship in Pi Beta Phi. 1867–1967* (Manesha, Wisconsin: George Banta Publishing, 1968), 172.
3. Ibid., 173.
4. Ibid., 184.
5. Ibid., 191–192.

APPENDIX

How to Date Quilts Made from 1925 to 1945

Characteristics of quilts made 1925–1945

Color: Color is one of the surest methods to date quilts from this era. Generally, as time went on, these quilts became softer in color; gone were the deep reds, blacks, browns, dark greens, purples, and navy blues of earlier quilts.

Solids: Clear pastels (robin's egg blue, lavender, pink, coral, medium green, yellow, and orange) were common in appliqué quilts especially.

Prints: Pastel prints with small-scale geometric, floral, and striped designs were set off against clean white background fabric in pieced and appliqué quilts.

Watch out! Some 1920s to 1940s quilts were made to look like nineteenth-century quilts. They *will* be made of solid fabrics in red, dark green, deep yellow, and pink. (See Washington's Plume, Illustration 3, as an example.) Even experts might mistake these quilts for their nineteenth-century models. The best advice is to check the green fabric. Twentieth-century green fabric will be lighter than the deep olive green of nineteenth-century fabric.

Patterns: Because of the heightened interest in quiltmaking during this period, quilt patterns entered the market by the hundreds. Old patterns were copied or updated, but original patterns were also developed. The most common patterns of the era were Flower Garden, Dresden Plate, and Wedding Ring.

Appliqué: Central Medallion appliqué quilts were common. Large baskets with realistic images of flowers, ribbons, and so forth are typical. These appliqués are most commonly made of solid-colored fabric. Blocks of appliqué designs were also possible. These designs are unfortunately not indexed in many quilt pattern encyclopedias. Check a few women's magazines and decorating magazines of the era at your local library. You may find your pattern.

Pieced: Pieced quilts in colorful print fabrics are the most common quilts of this era. Most pieced quilt patterns made in this era were printed in magazines or local newspapers. It is fun to track down patterns using microfilm readers if you have the time to spare. If not, consult one of the quilt pattern encyclopedias listed in the bibliography or contact a quilt researcher in your area.

String: String quilts made of small scraps of fabric were made before the 1920s. To identify 1920s to 1940s string quilts, look for the era's characteristic colors and fabrics. Unquilted string tops often still have their newspaper backings. Look for a date or a reported event to determine the date of the top. Even if the newspaper has been removed, look for small pieces of newspaper in the seams; you might find a date. When you do find one of these "dated" string quilts, use it as standard to determine the age of other quilts.

Embroidered: Often, printed quilt patterns included touches of embroidery, especially the outline stitch; but again check for the typical colors and fabrics of the 1920s to 1940s. Crazy quilts made of silk and velvet swatches also incorporated embroidery, but they had died out in popularity by 1920.

Cloth kits: A quilt kit might have included pre-cut and pre-sorted quilt pieces along with assembly instructions and background cloth stamped with appliqué placements and quilting lines. Some people have devalued these quilts, calling them simply "paint by number" projects. Others find them fascinating since they are definitely a sign of the times. Cloth kits were commonly sold by mail order during this period. More quilts than we realize may have been made from these kits. Without the actual kit box, you might look for blue placement lines under appliqué pieces. An unquilted top made from a kit will have tiny blue dots to mark the quilting pattern.

Shape: Quilts of this era often had scalloped edges bound in commercial bias tape. The bias binding has proven to be a reliable clue. A quilt with straight binding would more likely have been made in the nineteenth century. A quilt with a bias binding was probably made in the twentieth century.

Flour and Feed Sacks: Using printed trademarks and other information on sacks can help to date quilts made from them. By studying the history of textile bags, flour production, and sack printing, a quilt researcher can date quilts more easily. Sacks were used as quilt backings throughout the nineteenth century, but very few of those have printing left on them. By the 1920s, getting printed trademarks and advertising out of cotton sack cloth took several hours of hard work; fortunately for quilt researchers, many faded, but legible, trademarks remain on quilts.

What to look for:

1. Look for dates of copyright, printing, and packing. Record the names of the mills. Most have gone out of business, but you might be able to write to company officials asking for information when a particular design bag or logo was made.

2. Anna Cook discovered that bag manufacturers are a good source of information. Werthan Bag Company in Nashville told her that a series of numbers under their company logo refers to the printing date of the bag.

3. Look for bag company insignias that are often less obvious than the product logo. The logo for Bemis Bag is a cat coming out of a sack. Werthan Bag used a rooster.

4. On the Flour Mill Trademark Quilt (See illustration 90), there is a National Recovery Administration Blue Eagle, a symbol used only between May 1933 and May 1935, which aids in the dating of this anonymous quilt.

4. Flour measurements can also help to date the sack cloth. In the South, flour was sold in 96-pound, 48-pound, 24-pound, and 12-pound amounts. During World War II, the government standardized the sizes to one-hundred pounds, 50 pounds, and 25 pounds. So a quilt with a lining which still has its "24-pound" might have been made before World War II.

5. Unfortunately, no one has determined exactly when bag companies began glueing trademark labels to colorful print sacks. We know they were very popular during the 1930s; they continued to be popular well into the 1950s. Some printed cloth sacks are still sold.

6. Flour sack cloth is more tightly woven and smoother than chicken feed sacks. Sugar sacks were sheer, and rural quilters often used them as foundations for appliqué blocks (See illustration 116). However, similar cloth was available off the bolt in general stores. One of the best ways to determine if a quilt was made of sacks is to look for the telltale line of holes left when the heavy chain-stitched string was removed to open the sack.

You Can Help Preserve This History

Encourage descendants of quiltmakers to keep collections of printed materials, especially magazines, quilt catalogs, and patterns cut from newspapers. Or have them donate the materials to an appropriate organization.

Many quiltmakers kept their own collections of sample cloth blocks. Often the pattern and assembly instructions were attached. These collections are invaluable tools for dating quilts. Owners should compile the information and maintain the collections properly.

Record the stories of quiltmakers you meet, and photograph their quilts if permission is granted.

If you acquire a quilt, always ask for information on its background—maker, date made, pattern used, materials—and keep the information with the quilt, if possible.

PATTERNS

Four patterns from *Soft Covers for Hard Times* are included here for those who wish to make a Deparession-era quilt. Three methods for making templates are available. You can trace the shapes onto tissue paper; you can trace them onto sheets of clear plastic; or you can cut them out of heavy stock paper or sandpaper (the old-fashioned way).

Choose fabrics in colors you like. If you want the same effect as the quilt in the book, choose the same color values: dark, medium, or light. But don't try to copy the quilt exactly.

Place your template on the wrong side of the fabric and draw around it lightly with a quiltmaking pencil or chalk:

this is your stitching line. Then draw another line ¼-inch outside and parallel to the stitching line; this is your cutting line. The ¼-inch is your seam allowance.

Make one complete block before you cut out the rest of the pieces. This will let you see quickly if your fabric and color choices are satisfactory. For information on quilting and finishing a quilt, consult a local quilting guild or quilt shop owner.

Of the four blocks featured, Swing in the Center is the easiest, New York Beauty the most difficult. Four Tulips and Bull's Eye include a small amount of appliqué.

Swing in the Center
(as shown on page 19)

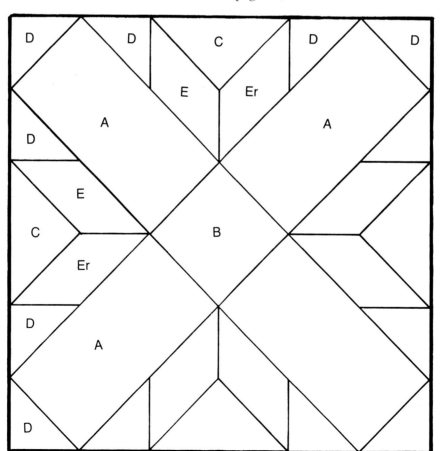

Completed block is 12 inches square.
Be sure to add ¼-inch seam allowance.

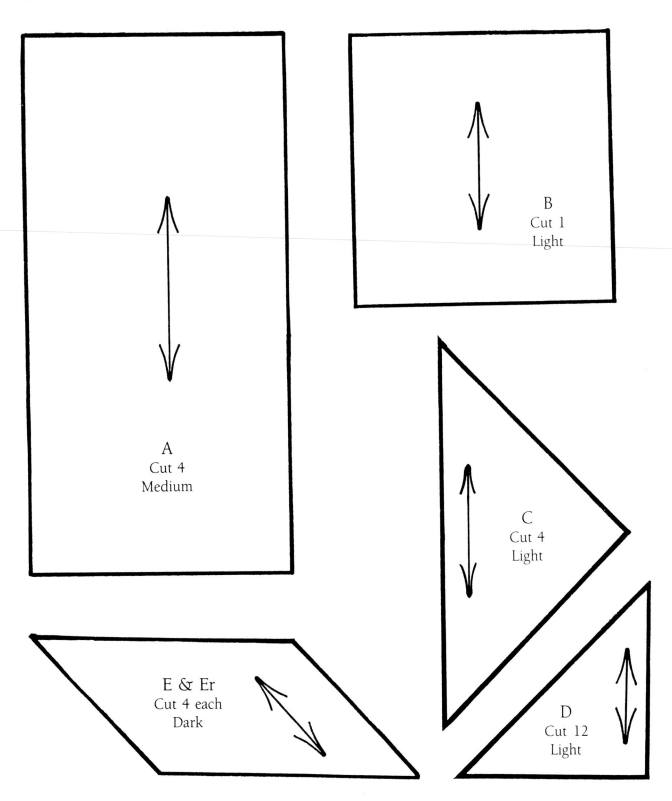

A
Cut 4
Medium

B
Cut 1
Light

C
Cut 4
Light

D
Cut 12
Light

E & Er
Cut 4 each
Dark

Four Tulips
(As shown on page 15)

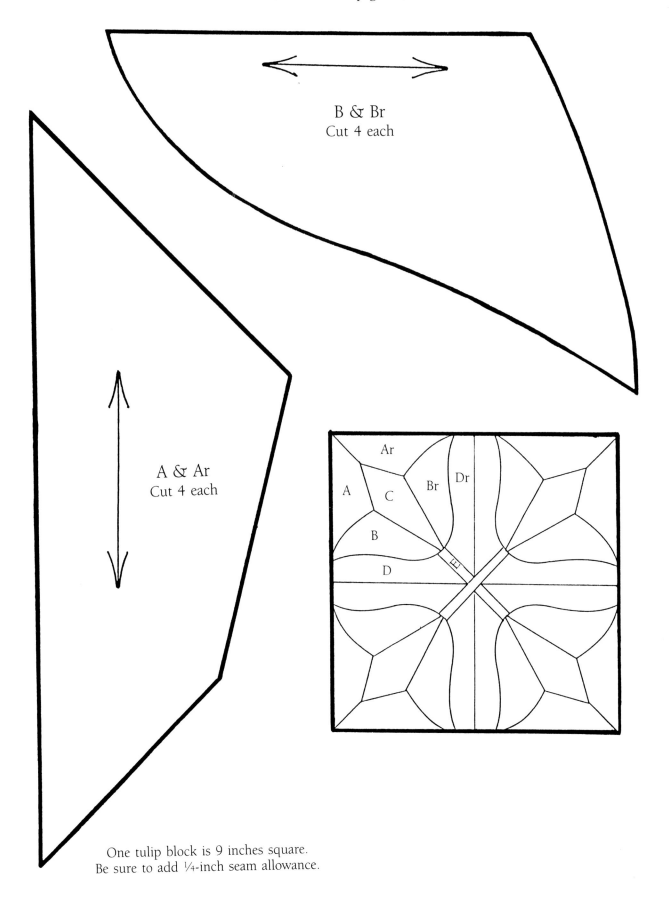

B & Br
Cut 4 each

A & Ar
Cut 4 each

Ar

A C Br Dr

B

D E

One tulip block is 9 inches square.
Be sure to add ¼-inch seam allowance.

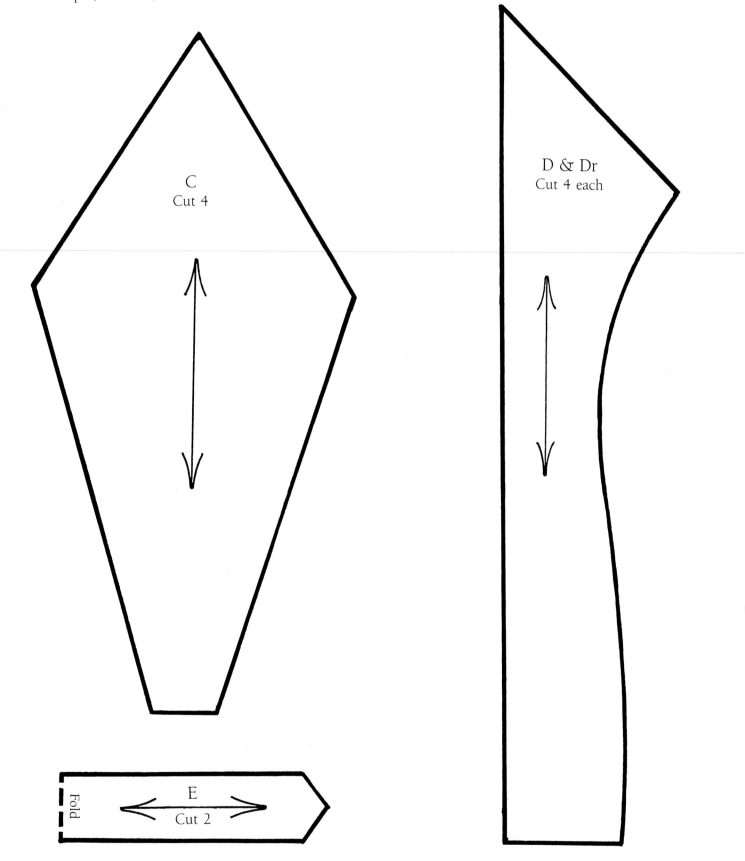

C
Cut 4

D & Dr
Cut 4 each

E
Cut 2

Fold

New York Beauty
(As shown on cover and page 21)

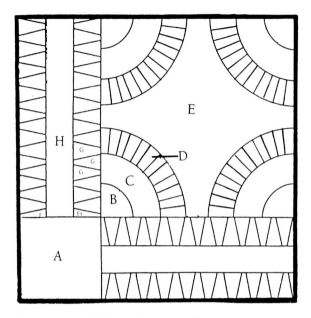

Be sure to add ¼-inch seam allowance.

Completed block is 17 inches square.

For accurage piecing, match up the center points on the
    curved pieces.

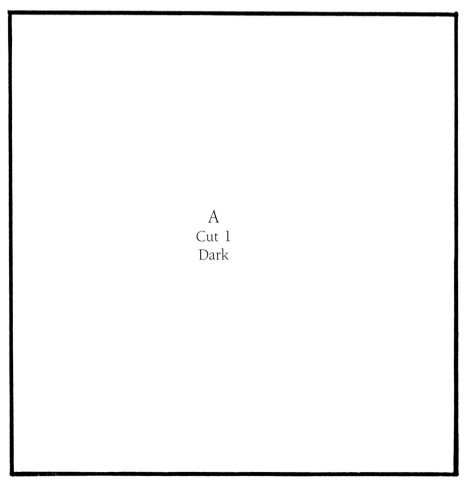

A
Cut 1
Dark

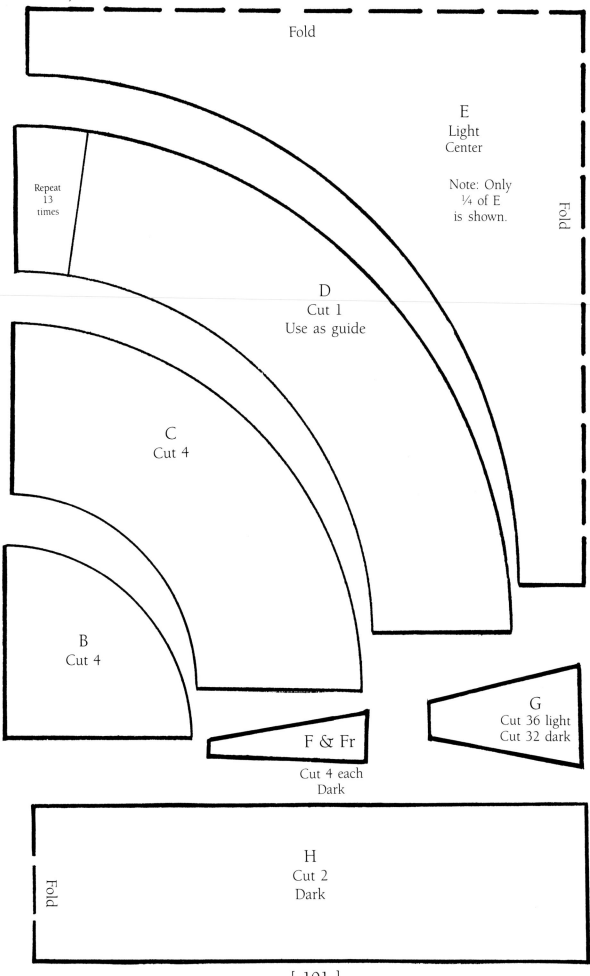

Fold

E
Light
Center

Note: Only
¼ of E
is shown.

Fold

Repeat
13
times

D
Cut 1
Use as guide

C
Cut 4

B
Cut 4

G
Cut 36 light
Cut 32 dark

F & Fr
Cut 4 each
Dark

H
Cut 2
Dark

Fold

Bull's Eye
(As shown on page 21)

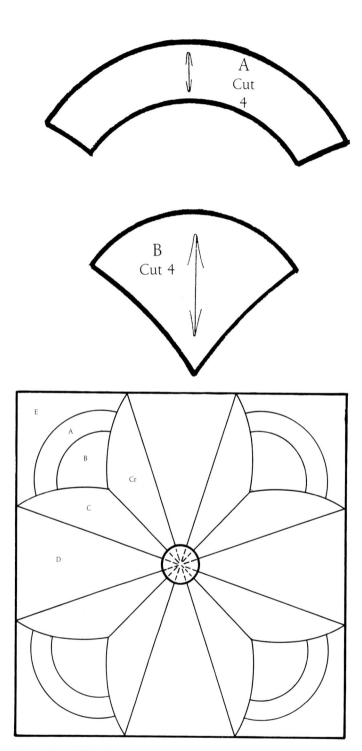

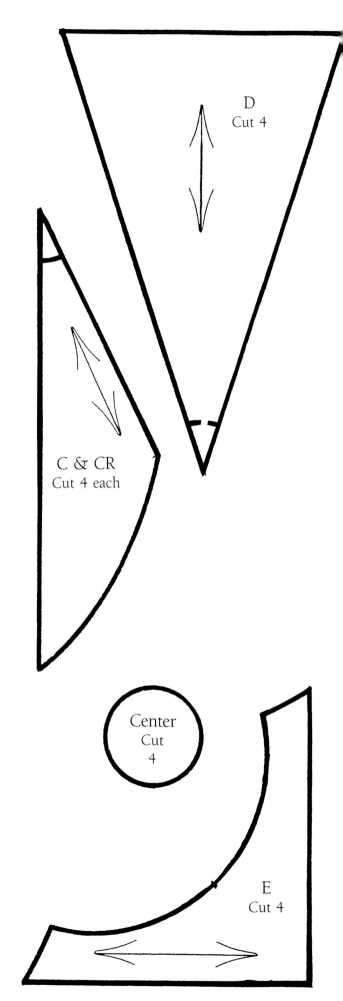

A
Cut 4

B
Cut 4

Cr

C

D

E

D
Cut 4

C & CR
Cut 4 each

Center
Cut
4

E
Cut 4

Completed block is 9 inches square.
Be sure to add ¼-inch seam allowance.
For accurate piecing, match up the center points on the
    curved pieces.
Appliqué the center circles.

GLOSSARY

Appliqué: laid-on pieces of cloth sewed to a background material.

Backing: material used as the underside of the quilt.

Baste: to join the layers of the quilt together using long, loose stitches in preparation for the quilting process.

Batt: a small unit of cotton filler combed by hand or by wire brushes called cards; a commercially prepared full-size filler for a quilt.

Batting: the padding or filler of a quilt.

Binding: finish for the raw edge of the quilt, done with a strip of straight or bias material.

Block: a unit or section of a quilt made of joined pieces or of background material with applied pieces.

Border: solid, pieced, or appliquéd band at outer edge of quilt or surrounding center medallion.

Boss Ball thread: very heavy cotton thread used for piercing and quilting.

Brown Domestic: a name for muslin cloth.

Carding: combing the cotton or wool with wire brushes to prepare it for spinning or for quilt filler.

Center or Central Medallion: central motif of a quilt design surrounded by borders or other units.

Design: the overall organization of a quilt or a specific pattern.

Domestic: a name for muslin cloth.

Elbow Quilting: allover design of arc rows of quilting. The elbow can act as a compass point in drawing the major arc.

Fan Quilting: (see preceding entry).

Filling: the padding of a quilt, usually cotton or wool, placed between the top and bottom fabric of the quilt.

Frame (or quilting frame): basically four strips of wood in rectangular shape to which is fastened the three layers of the quilt prior to quilting.

Lining: backing or underside of a quilt.

Pattern: the design unit of a quilt.

Patchwork: pieces of fabric seamed together, as in pieced work or applied to a background, as in appliqué, and joined together to make a whole.

Pieced Work: joining pieces by seaming together to make a whole, usually in geometric design.

Quilt: two layers of cloth with padding between, stitched or tied together.

Quilting: stitching through layers of fabric and padding.

Remnants: short lengths of fabrics.

Sashing: band added between blocks in joining.

Set: the material used, as well as the arrangement of joining blocks.

Shell Quilting: (see "Elbow Quilting").

Stamp: to print a pattern on cloth.

Stamping Outfit: a commercial device used by quiltmakers to transfer quilting lines to quilt tops.

String: a small scrap of fabric.

String Piecing: the joining of narrow strips, usually in random size, to a foundation of paper or cloth to make a unit.

Template: a pattern, usually in the form of cardboard, to assure accuracy in cutting quilt block pieces.

Top: the upper and outer layer of a quilt.

Transfer Pattern: a tissue paper pattern printed with a special type of ink.

Transfer Process: to duplicate exactly a pattern's pieces on cloth or another piece of paper, usually by passing a hot iron over the paper pattern placed inkside down.

Wholecloth: quilt top of solid material, often three panels seamed together and quilted.

LENDERS &
INTERVIEWEES

LENDERS

Allene Blalock
Ruth Clement Bond
Tracy Brown
Susan Visconage Buerkens
Clara Carmichael
La Delle Reagan Compton
Anna Lue Cook
Emily Daniel Cox
Dot Davis
Frances Dunlap
H. L. Durrett
Beth Dyer
Sherry Edwards
Hilary Goldstine
Edna Gossage
Don Graham
Lois Hall

Kay Hardy
Gordon Irwin
Eva Earle Kent
Bernice Schultz Mackey
Georgia Thomas Mize
Reba Johnson Parham
Becky Salmond
Rose Marie Thomas
Virginia Reed Tobias
Grace Tyler
Inez Ward
Jeanne Gilmore Webb
Viola Webb
Mable Marshall Westbrooks
Frances Whittemore
Rachel Huff Wilson
Rebecca DeWitt Wright

INTERVIEWEES

Depression Era Quiltmakers:

Polly Dixon

Edna Gossage

Mattie Jane Haun

Willie Emert Hogerty

Euretha Irwin

Nora Crabtree Ladd

Bernice Schultz Mackey

Georgia Thomas Mize

Reba Johnson Parham

Pauline Pruitt

Sarah Raley

Ruth Reed

Lucille Sanders

Georgia Swanner

Vacie Thomas

Inez Ward

Viola Webb

Maude Wise

Descendants and Acquaintances:

Allene Blalock

Sally Cavin

Susan Ciebell

La Delle Reagan Compton

Emily Daniel Cox

Frances Davies

Margaret Blackman Davis

John DeWitt Jr.

Frances Dunlap

Louise Edelman

Claire Gilbert

Lois Hall

Susie Irwin

Phoebe Mann

Sally Mae Rice

Mary Rockette

Virginia Sanders

Margaret Trudel

Shirley Visconage

Dorothy Watt

Jeanne Gilmore Webb

Mable Westbrooks

Frances Whittemore

Rachel Huff Wilson

Rebecca DeWitt Wright

Anne Orr's Family and Friends:

Anne Callahan

Glenda Grigsby

J. Scott Grigsby

Jean Oldfield

Andrena Phillips

Tennessee Valley Authority Quilts:

Ruth Clement Bond

J. Max Bond

Li Fran Fort

Walter Golston

Ralph Martin

Elizabeth Martinson

Rose Marie Thomas

Grace Tyler

Flour Mills and Sacks:

H. L. Durrett

Mike Durrett

Ted Pedas

Robert Schuey

Albert Werthan

BIBLIOGRAPHY

Axelrod, Alan (ed.). *The Colonial Revival in America*. New York: W. W. Norton & Company, 1985.

Bird, Caroline. *The Invisible Scar*. New York: David McKay Company, 1966.

Blanchard, Rebecca Marie Trahan. *Missouri Quilts of the 1930s*. M.A. Thesis, University of Missouri-Columbia. 1987.

Brackman, Barbara. *An Encyclopedia of Pieced Quilt Patterns*. 8 vols. Lawrence, Kansas: Prairie Flower Publishing, 1979–1983.

Brackman, Barbara. *Clues in the Calico: A Guide to Identifying and Dating Antique Quilts*. Alexandria, Virginia: EPM Publications, Inc., 1989.

Brackman, Barbara. "Looking Back at the Great Quilt Contest." *Quilter's Newsletter* 156: 22–24.

Brackman, Barbara. "Quilts at Chicago's World's Fairs" in *Uncoverings 1981*. Mill Valley, California: American Quilt Study Group, 1982, 63–76.

Bresenhan, Karoline, and Nancy O'Bryant Puentes. *Lone Stars: A Legacy of Texas Quilts, 1836–1936*.

Burdick, Nancilu B. *Legacy: The Story of Talula Gilbert Bottoms and Her Quilts*. Nashville: Rutledge Hill Press, 1988.

Clarke, Mary Washington. *Kentucky Quilts and Their Makers*. Lexington, Kentucky: The University of Kentucky Press, 1976.

Cooper, Patricia, and Norma Bradley Buferd. *The Quilters: Women and Domestic Art*. Garden City, New York: Anchor Press, 1978.

Dubois, Jean. *Anne Orr Patchwork*. Durango, Colorado: La Plata Press, 1977.

Dunton, William Rush, Jr. *Old Quilts*. Cantonsville, Maryland: privately printed, 1946.

Eaton, Allen H. *Handicrafts of the Southern Highlands: A Book on Rural Arts*. New York: Russell Sage Foundation, 1937.

Elwood, Judy, Joyce Tennery, and Alice Richardson. *Tennessee Quilting: Designs Plus Patterns*. Oak Ridge: privately printed, 1982.

Finley, Ruth E. *Old Patchwork Quilts and the Women Who Made Them,* 1929. Reprint. Newton Center, Massachusetts: Charles T. Branford Co., 1970.

Freedman, Estelle B. *Their Sisters' Keepers: Women's Prison Reform in America, 1830–1930*. Ann Arbor: University of Michigan Press, 1981.

Freeman, Roland. *Something to Keep You Warm*. Jackson, Mississippi: Mississippi Department of Archives and History, 1981.

Garoutte, Sally, ed. *Uncoverings*. Mill Valley, California: American Quilt Study Group, 1980–1986.

Grant, Nancy. *Blacks, Regional Planning, and The TVA*. University of Chicago dissertation. 1978.

Hall, Carrie A., and Rose G. Kretsinger. *The Romance of the Patchwork Quilt in America*. New York: Bonanza Books, 1935.

Havig, Bettina. *Missouri Heritage Quilts*. Paducah, Kentucky: The American Quilter's Society, 1986.

Holstein, Jonathan. *The Pieced Quilt: An American Design Tradition,* Greenwich, Connecticut: New York Graphic Society, Ltd., 1973.

Horton, Laurel, ed. *Uncoverings*. Mill Valley, California: American Quilt Study Group, 1987–1988.

Horwitz, Elinor Lander. *Mountain People, Mountain Crafts*. Philadelphia: J. B. Lippincott Co., 1974.

Ickis, Marguerite. *The Standard Book of Quilt Making and Collecting*. 1949. Reprint. New York: Dover Publications, Inc., 1959.

Irwin, John Rice. *A People and Their Quilts*. Exton, Pennsylvania: Schiffer Publishing Ltd., 1983.

Lasansky, Jeannette. *In the Heart of Pennsylvania: 19th and 20th Century Quiltmaking Traditions*. Lewisburg, Pennsylvania: Oral Traditions Project of the Union County Historical Society, 1985.

Lasansky, Jeannett, ed. *Pieced by Mother: Symposium Papers*. Lewisburg, Pennsylvania: Oral Traditions Project of Union County Historical Society, 1988.

MacDowell, Marsha, and Ruth D. Fitzgerald, ed. *Michigan Quilts: 150 Years of a Textile Tradition*. East Lansing, Michigan: Michigan State University, 1987.

McDonald, Michael J., and John Muldowny. *TVA and the Dispossessed*. Knoxville: University of Tennessee Press, 1982.

McKim, Ruby S. *101 Patchwork Patterns*. 2nd ed. New York: Dover Publications, Inc., 1962.

Marshall, Martha. *Quilts of Appalachia: The Mountain Woman and Her Quilts.* Bluff City, Tennessee: Tri-City Printing Co., 1972.

Minton, John Dean. *The New Deal in Tennessee: 1932–1938.* New York: Garland Publishing, 1979.

Nickols, Pat. "String Quilts." In *Uncoverings 1982.* Mill Valley, California: American Quilt Study Group, 1983.

Nickols, Pat. "The Use of Cotton Sacks in Quiltmaking." In *Uncoverings 1988.* San Francisco, California: American Quilt Study Group, 1989.

Oklahoma Quilt Heritage Project. *Oklahoma Heritage Quilts: A Sampling of Quilts Made in or Brought to Oklahoma before 1940.* Paducah, Kentucky: American Quilter's Society, 1990.

Orlofsky, Patsy, and Myron Orlofsky. *Quilts in America.* New York: McGraw Hill Book Co., 1974.

Puckett, Marjorie. *String Quilts 'n Things.* Orange, California: Orange Patchwork Publishers, 1979.

Rafter, Nicole Hahn. *Partial Justice: Women in State Prisons 1800–1935.* Boston: Northeastern University Press, 1985.

Ramsey, Bets, ed. *Quilt Close-Up: Five Southern Views.* Chattanooga, Tennessee: The Hunter Museum of Art, 1983.

Ramsey, Bets. *Old and New Quilt Patterns in the Southern Tradition.* Nashville: Rutledge Hill Press, 1987.

Ramsey, Bets, and Merikay Waldvogel. *The Quilts of Tennessee: Images of Domestic Life Prior to 1930.* Nashville: Rutledge Hill Press, 1986.

Roberson, Ruth H., ed. *North Carolina Quilts.* Chapel Hill, North Carolina: University of North Carolina Press, 1988.

Safford, Carleton L., and Robert Bishop. *America's Quilts and Coverlets.* New York: E. P. Dutton & Co., Inc., 1972.

Steen, Herman. *Flour Milling in America.* Westport, Connecticut: Greenwood Press, 1963.

Twelker, Nancyann Johanson. *Women and Their Quilts: A Washington State Centennial Tribute.* Bothell, Washington: That Patchwork Place, Inc., 1988.

Webster, Marie D. *Quilts: Their Story and How to Make Them.* New York: Doubleday, Page and Co., 1926.

Wilson, Sadye Tune, and Doris Finch Kennedy. *Of Coverlets: The Legacies, the Weavers.* Nashville, Tennessee: Tunstede, 1983.

Woodard, Thomas K., and Blanche Greenstein. *Twentieth Century Quilts 1900–1950.* New York: E. P. Dutton, 1988.

Yabsley, Suzanne. *Texas Quilts, Texas Women.* College Station, Texas: Texas A & M University Press, 1984.

Index

advertising, xiii, 16, 40
African American quiltmakers, 21, 78–82
African-American music, xiv
Agricultural Extension Service, xiii
Alabama, 78, 79, 82
American Quilt Study Group, 92
Andersonville, Tennessee, 29, 35
Anne Orr Patchwork, 34
Appalachian craft industry, xiv
appliqué placement guides, 7, 12, 14, 32, 35
appliqué quilts, xiv, 2, 4–6, 7, 8, 11, 12, 13, 16, 22–23, 27, 28, 34, 41, 43, 44, 47, 52, 59, 79, 80–81, 82
The Arrow, 99
Arrowcraft Shop, 83
Arrowcraft Weaving Quilt, 84
Arrowmont School of Arts and Crafts, 83
art education, 30
Arts and Crafts Movement, xii
Ascension Self Rising Flour, 65
Aster, 30
Atlanta Constitution, 44
Atlanta, Georgia, 40, 44, 81
atomic bomb, development of, 60
Aunt Lizzie Reagan, 83–84
Autumn Leaf, 32

bag manufacturers, 91; marketing techniques, 64, 67
Ballard Chefs, xiii
Ballard Flour Mills, xiii
Baptist Church, 41, 60
Barding, Mary Ellen, 57
bartering, 60
Basket, 75; 73–74
Basket and Blossom, 2–3; full view, 13
Basket of Flowers, 6; full view, 7
batting, xii, 57
Bear Paw, 9
Belmont College, 41
Bemis Bag Company, 65, 67
Benberry, Cuesta, 30, 35
binding a quilt, 74
Black Power Quilt, 78, 81, 92
black quiltmakers, 21, 78–82
Blalock, Allene, 17
blue eagle, 66, 85
blue grass music, xiv

Bond, George Clement, 78; J. Max, Jr., 78; Max, 78; Jane, 78, 80, 82; Bond, Ruth Clement, 78–82, 92
boss ball thread, 55, 70–71
Boston, 40
Bougereau, Julien, 35, 41
Bow Knot, 32
Bride's Quilt, 41–42
Briscoe, Mrs. Daniel, 42
broadcloth, 52, 54
Broken Star, 4 (caption)
Broken Star, 54, 4; (caption), 52
Brown Cow Feed, 64
Brown, Annie Belle Hodges 57; Tracy, 57
Brownsville Fundraising Quilt, 60; full view, 61
Brownsville, Tennessee, 60–61
Buerkens, Susan Visconage, 43
Bull's Eye, 21
burlap sacks, 57
Burnett, Beth, 46
Burrus Mills, xiv
Busby Berkeley, xiv
Bussey, Ezra, 30; Mary, 30
Butler, George, 12

Caden Art Shop, xii–xiii
Caden, Margaret Rogers, xii–xiv, 40, 46
California, 46
Callahan, Anne, 37
Carden, Bonnie, 29
Carl Junction, Missouri, 32
Carmichael, Clara, 21
Carnation Flour, 67
central medallion quilt, 4, 7, 15, 20, 28, 29, 32, 94
Century of Progress Contest (See Sears National Quilt Contest)
Century of Progress Quilt, 38–39; full view, 43
Century of Progress theme quilts, 40, 44
Chapman, Katherine Hopkins, 26
Chase Bag Company, 67
Chattanooga Times, 18
Chattanooga, Tennessee, 50
Chicago Art Institute, 42
Chicago World's Fair 1893, xii

Chicago World's Fair 1933, xii–xiii, xiv, 7, 32, 38, 42, 44
Chicago, Illinois, 10, 14, 16, 20, 32, 36, 40
china painting, 37
Ciebell, Susan, 30
Cincinnati, Ohio, 20
Civil War, 41, 62
Civilian Conservation Corps, 76, 89
Clark Thread Company, 26
Clark, W. L. M., 10
Clarksville, Tennessee, 6, 67
Clement, Emma, 78; George C., 78
Clifty Community, Tennessee, 51
Clinton, Tennessee, 88
cloth kit, 4 (caption), 14, 20, 52, 54, 94
Coats, J. P. Thread Company, 26
Cogswell, Robert, xiv
Colonial Quilt Book, 20
Colonial Revival, ix, xii–xiii, 10, 23, 37, 47, 48
Colonial Revival quilts, 4–5, 7, 11
Colonial Sugar, 64, 65
color-fast fabrics, 48
Columbia, Tennessee, 7
Comfort, 14
Commercial Appeal, 20
commercial patterns, 6, 12, 14, 16, 19, 20, 21, 22; source of, 20, 24
commercialization, xiv
competitions, national, xiii
Compton, La Delle Reagan, 83–84
Conley, Sarah Ward, 35, 41
contests, judging ethics, 32
Continental Quilting Congress, 24
cooperative programs, 86
Cope, James, 12; Susie, 12
Cosmos, 27
cottage industries, xiii
Cotton Bag Loan Wardrobe, 67
cotton, growing for quilts, 57
Cottrell, Frenchy, 92
country music, xiii–xiv, 58
Cox, Amy, 88
crafts, traditional, 78, 83–84, 88
crazy quilts, 2
crochet patterns, 26–27
Cross Stitch Bouquet, 34
Cross Stitch Designs Set J, 26

[108]